POPULAR DAY HIKES

Jasper
Mount Robson—Valemount—Yellowhead Highway

POPULAR DAY HIKES

Jasper
Mount Robson
Valemount
Yellowhead Highway

Ben
Nearingburg

RMB

For information on purchasing bulk quantities of this book, or to obtain media excerpts or invite the author to speak at an event, please visit rmbooks.com and select the "Contact" tab.

RMB | Rocky Mountain Books Ltd.
rmbooks.com
@rmbooks
facebook.com/rmbooks

Cataloguing data available from Library and Archives Canada
ISBN 9781771606950 (softcover)
ISBN 9781771606967 (electronic)

All photographs are by Ben Nearingburg unless otherwise noted.

Printed and bound in China

We would like to also take this opportunity to acknowledge the Traditional Territories upon which we live and work. In Calgary, Alberta, we acknowledge the Niitsítapi (Blackfoot) and the people of the Treaty 7 region in Southern Alberta, which includes the Siksika, the Piikuni, the Kainai, the Tsuut'ina and the Stoney Nakoda First Nations, including Chiniki, Bearpaw, and Wesley First Nations. The City of Calgary is also home to Métis Nation of Alberta, Region III. In Victoria, British Columbia, we acknowledge the Traditional Territories of the Lkwungen (Esquimalt, and Songhees), Malahat, Pacheedaht, Scia'new, T'Sou-ke and W̱SÁNEĆ (Pauquachin, Tsartlip, Tsawout, Tseycum) peoples.

We acknowledge the financial support of the Government of Canada through the Canada Book Fund and the Canada Council for the Arts, and of the province of British Columbia through the British Columbia Arts Council and the Book Publishing Tax Credit.

Disclaimer
The actions described in this book are considered inherently dangerous activities. Individuals undertake these activities at their own risk. The information put forth in this guide has been collected from a variety of sources and is not guaranteed to be completely accurate or reliable. Route conditions and some information may change owing to weather and numerous other factors beyond the control of the authors and publishers. Individuals or groups must determine the risks, use their own judgement, and take full responsibility for their actions. Do not depend on any information found in this book for your own personal safety. Your safety depends on your own good judgement based on your skills, education, and experience.

It is up to the users of this guidebook to acquire the necessary skills for safe experiences and to exercise caution in potentially hazardous areas. The authors and publishers of this guide accept no responsibility for your actions or the results that occur from another's actions, choices, or judgements. If you have any doubt as to your safety or your ability to attempt anything described in this guidebook, do not attempt it.

Contents

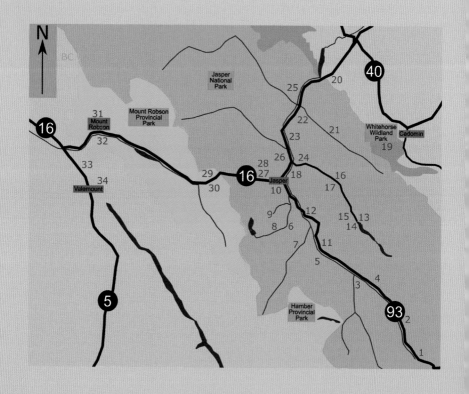

Introduction

There are few more sought-after hiking destinations than the Canadian Rockies. With towering peaks, pristine lakes and serene forests there is a lifetime's worth of terrain to explore. This book focuses on a more northerly stretch of the Rockies, including Jasper National Park, Mount Robson Provincial Park and a few additional areas to the east and west. Hikers of all ages and abilities will find exciting and enchanting trails with plenty of opportunities for wildflower viewing and wildlife sightings.

Using this book

Variety, popularity and beauty are the three core factors uniting the routes in this book. Routes were chosen to give a broad range of difficulty and duration while staying within the scope of a day hike.

Trails

The trails described are generally well equipped, with informative trailhead kiosks and large parking areas. Several indistinct or confusing sections, particularly above treeline, are highlighted in route descriptions and often marked by small cairns or flagging tape. Most of the trails in this book are multi-use, and do not be surprised to see mountain bikers, horse parties and animal traffic.

Difficulty

Trails in this book are graded in two different ways. First, the overall challenge of the route is rated as Easy, Moderate or Strenuous. Second, the specific types of terrain encountered are described, along with any relevant hazards.

Distances

Distances, unless indicated otherwise, are round trip (i.e., car to car), not including any described optional extensions. All distances were gathered using a professional GPS device, and averaged over several measurements. Values may differ from those found on Parks Canada maps.

Height gain

The total elevation gain for each trail is listed and refers to the total round trip, car to car, unless indicated otherwise.

Hazards or regulations

Pay special attention to any red text, which describes exceptional hazards or specific regulations.

Options

Many of the described routes have optional extensions or variations. Look for *Going Farther* headings, which describe these options with added distance, height gain and difficulty information.

Sketch maps

Each route has a rough map showing the local area and relevant features. The main trail is shown as a solid red line. Dotted red lines indicate optional extensions or other nearby trails. Waypoints are shown as red dots, with distances between waypoints also given. The elevation contour interval is 40 metres unless indicated otherwise.

Do I need other maps?

If you stay on the described trails, it is unlikely you would need any additional maps. However, it is highly recommended to also carry a combination navigation/interpretation map such as the Gem Trek® series. Maps help to identify distant peaks, plan future adventures and generally orient yourself in the wider landscape. There are many stores in Jasper that sell maps of various sizes and resolutions. Digital mapping products such as Gaia GPS®, Topo Maps Canada® etc. can be very useful and are also recommended.

Getting to the trailhead

The area map following the Contents page shows the main highways to get to the trails described. Trailhead directions are given starting from the intersection of Hwy 93 (the Icefields Parkway) and Hwy 16 (the Yellowhead Highway) south of Jasper (the likely basecamp for most visitors to the region). While several trails around the townsite could be accessed by foot or bike, having a vehicle is strongly advised.

Weather

The Canadian Rockies are known for long, chilly winters and short, warm summers. Typically, early July to mid-September is the best season for hiking, with daily highs averaging in the mid-20s. (The highest temperature ever officially recorded in Jasper was 41.2°C, in late June 2020, while the coldest was –47.2°C, in January 1916.) Considerable snowfall at higher elevations means that many alpine trails remain snowbound until July. By late October, winter creeps back to the hills and hikers will trade their boots for skis and snowshoes. Hikers should be prepared for rapidly changing mountain weather, and afternoon thunderstorms are particularly common throughout the summer months.

What to wear for the trails

Since mountain weather can change very quickly, proper clothing is key to being prepared. Start with breathable synthetic (i.e., non-cotton) base layers and add insulating and waterproof layers as required. Any time there is rain in the forecast or if your route will take you above treeline, a waterproof jacket and pants are highly recommended. It's also a good idea to carry sunscreen and insect repellent. Light hiking boots are recommended for all of the routes in this book.

Drinking water

Potable water is available in Jasper, at roadside lodges and in many of the frontcountry campgrounds. Surface water sources across the region (creeks, rivers and lakes) should be properly treated (i.e., by following an approved method such as filtering, boiling, UV sterilization etc.) before consumption. It is highly recommended to keep a large water jug in your car, particularly on hot summer days.

Wildlife concerns

While being a popular destination for tourism, the Canadian Rockies are also home to many creatures, both tall and small. Animals that may be encountered during your travels include (but are not limited to) deer, elk, moose, Rocky Mountain bighorn sheep, mountain goats, black bears and grizzly bears. Parks Canada recommends keeping at least 30 m of distance between yourself and any ungulates (deer, elk, moose) and at least 100 m between yourself and any bears. Elk and moose should be given extra space during the fall mating season. Best practices for travelling are to stay in larger groups and make plenty of noise to alert animals to your presence. Adults should carry bear spray and be comfortable using it.

Dogs on trails

Many of the trails described in this book are located in woodland caribou habitat; dogs are strictly banned from these areas. If in doubt, look for references in trail descriptions as well as on signage at trailhead kiosks. Elsewhere in the park, dogs must be kept on leash.

Camping

For those budget conscious (or more adventurous) travellers, camping is a great way to experience more Rocky Mountain ambience. Frontcountry campgrounds are spread across the region and can be reserved by contacting Parks Canada, Alberta Parks or BCParks. While limited amounts of first-come, first-served camping are available in the region, vacant sites can be scarce during the popular summer months and reservations are highly recommended.

Supplies

The main hub for supplies, accommodations, gear and trinkets in this region is the Jasper townsite. Limited facilities (including restaurants and gift shops) also exist in the Maligne Valley. Down the Icefields Parkway there are frontcountry campgrounds, roadside hostels, roadside lodges and one gas station. East of town there are several roadside lodges within the park, and all services are available in the neighbouring community of Hinton, an hour's drive east of Jasper. West of Jasper, in Mount Robson Provincial Park, there are frontcountry campgrounds as well a small café and gas station beside the visitor centre.

Doing more

This book serves as a great introduction to the region. But there are many more trails to explore, particularly deeper into the backcountry as part of multi-day trips. Some recommended publications with inspiration for longer routes include *Canadian Rockies Trail Guide*, by Brian Patton and Bart Robinson, and *Jasper–Robson: A Taste of Heaven*, by Don Beers. Though the latter title is now out of print, it is still, in my opinion, the most comprehensive reference for the less-travelled trails in the region.

To expand adventures into the long winter months, there are cross-country and alpine ski-touring routes described in *Ski Trails in the Canadian Rockies*, by Chic Scott and Darren Farley.

Strong hikers who are looking to expand their horizons should consider branching into scrambling (i.e., venturing into steeper and more committing terrain but still not needing ropes or technical gear). There are a vast number of peaks and ridges that can be ascended by scrambling techniques, offering literally years of adventure. It is highly recommended to join a mentoring organization such as the Alpine Club of Canada or to pursue formal backcountry education with a certified guide from the Association of Canadian Mountain Guides before setting off on a scrambling career. Good scrambling references for the region include *Scrambles in the Canadian Rockies*, by Alan Kane, and *A Peakbagger's Guide to the Canadian Rockies: North*, by Ben Nearingburg and Eric Coulthard.

Geraldine Falls

SOUTH OF TOWN; ICEFIELDS PARKWAY

1 Wilcox Pass to Tangle Falls

An exceptionally scenic extension to the popular Wilcox Pass trail which maximizes time spent in the alpine. While this route is described here as a traverse (and works best with a car staged at each end), it also makes for a fine day trip to start at the Wilcox Pass trailhead, traverse the pass and return that same way.

DISTANCE: 12 KM ONE WAY

HEIGHT GAIN: 500 METRES ONE WAY

HIGH POINT: 2380 METRES

STRENUOUS

MID-JULY TO THE END OF SEPTEMBER

Start: North terminus: Tangle Falls parking area. From the junction of Hwys 16 and 93 near Jasper, travel south for 95 km and turn right into the signed parking area on the west side of the highway. South terminus: Wilcox campground road. From the Junction of Hwys 16 and 93 near Jasper, travel south for 105 km, past the Icefield Centre, and turn left at the signed campground on the east side of the highway.

Difficulty: A rocky and rooted trail for the first 3.7 km to reach Wilcox Pass. After the pass, the trail becomes less distinct, even overgrown in places, but still easy to follow.

1. Leaving the trailhead kiosk, the route starts climbing and quickly comes to an unsigned junction before a shallow lake. Over the next 450 m the trail gains elevation consistently. You will encounter many roots and a well-made set of stairs as you travel upwards before emerging to a great trailside viewpoint.

2. After the viewpoint, carry on upwards as the forest thins and you'll reach an iconic "red chairs" viewpoint overlooking Athabasca Glacier. Where several spur trails lead downwards to the left, stay on the main path. Those spurs eventually descend to the Icefields campground, but they are steep, bushy and not recommended. Some 500 m after leaving the red chairs, a change in vegetation announces your arrival into the alpine. Be sure to stay on the main trail, even if it is muddy, to avoid damaging the fragile alpine environment. Signage for Wilcox Pass (at 2370 metres elevation) is 2 km from the "red-chair" viewpoint, with a small, shallow creek crossing just before it.

3. At the pass, a trail sign points to the Wilcox Ridge viewpoint (see extension below). The main route continues northwards and crosses a wilderness trail sign before winding through the open meadows of the pass, staying near the base of Wilcox Peak. At 2.9 km the trail passes through a rockslide; look for cairns pointing the way across to the well-defined trail on the north side.

4. Some 1.5 km past the rockslide, the open alpine travel draws to a close and the trail switchbacks down into the Tangle Creek valley. While the trail is still very well defined, it can be overgrown in places, and

◀ *The start of the trail can be quite rooty, but travel is swift.*

if the foliage is damp with morning dew or recent rain, putting on rain pants is highly recommended.

5. The trail follows Tangle Creek until it reaches a flagged junction at the route for Tangle Ridge. Stay left on the main trail, which soon leaves the creek and enters denser forest. After several steep switchbacks, you'll encounter remnants of an old outfitter cabin before coming to a spectacular viewpoint of peaks of the Columbia Icefield. After several more switchbacks the trail reaches an old roadbed which leads to the Tangle Falls parking area and the end of the traverse.

▲ Looking up towards the outlier of Nigel Peak from a tranquil trailside pond.

▼ Perched across the valley from Athabasca Glacier, these red chairs offer one of the most majestic roadside views in Jasper National Park.

▲ Once in the alpine, there are stunning views of peaks and glaciers in all directions. Mount Athabasca (centre) is one of the most photographed peaks in the Canadian Rockies and a classic destination for mountaineers.

▼ Looking north across Wilcox Pass at the viewpoint junction. Mount Wilcox rises on the left, and Tangle Ridge is visible far in the distance (centre).

▼ Excellent views continue farther along Wilcox Pass as Tangle Ridge (left) starts to loom larger and distant peaks around Beauty Lakes (distant centre) also come into view.

▲ This old bridge is emblematic of the trail after descending from Wilcox Pass. While still very easy to follow, the route can be overgrown in places.

▼ Beautiful views towards Mount Kitchener (centre) and Stutfield Peak (right) before the trail descends to the highway.

Going farther: Wilcox Viewpoint

For more great views of Athabasca Glacier, it is worthwhile adding this short side trip to the Wilcox Viewpoint.

DISTANCE: ADD 2.8 KM RETURN (FROM WILCOX PASS SIGN)

HEIGHT GAIN: 100 METRES RETURN (FROM WILCOX PASS SIGN)

HIGH POINT: 2400 METRES

1. The route to the Wilcox Ridge viewpoint is well marked with yellow-diamond signs mounted in gabions (rocks bound together in a metal mesh). From the Wilcox Pass sign, head upwards as the trail climbs over two small ridges with great views towards Mount Wilcox and Mount Athabasca.

2. After the second ridge, the trail descends to a seasonal creek, then regains elevation and hooks slightly to the right as it leads to a rocky outcrop overlooking the Columbia Icefield Discovery Centre and the rest of the Columbia Icefield area.

3. Retrace your steps back to the Wilcox Pass junction.

▲ *Even the relatively minor elevation gain of the viewpoint trail is enough to give a great perspective on Wilcox Pass.*

▼ *Yellow diamond markers point the way along the viewpoint trail as it winds its way towards Athabasca Glacier. The official lookout is far in the distance.*

2 Tangle Ridge

One of the premier viewpoints along the Icefields Parkway, perfectly located for views of peaks bordering the Columbia Icefield. This is a steep and sustained hike, and once it passes into the alpine, the route travels off-trail on easy scree to reach the summit.

DISTANCE: 10.8 KM

HEIGHT GAIN: 1150 METRES

HIGH POINT: 3000 METRES

STRENUOUS

MID-JULY TO LATE SEPTEMBER

Start: Tangle Falls parking area. From the Junction of Hwys 16 and 93 near Jasper, travel south for 95 km and turn right, into the signed parking area on the west side of the highway.

Difficulty: A steep, rooted and rocky trail which includes one unbridged creek crossing. From parking area to treeline the trail is wide and easy to follow; above treeline, easy off-trail scree leads to the summit.

1. While the signed trailhead is visible from the road, it is a bit camouflaged with foliage. Use the crosswalk and gain the embankment on the right (south) side of Tangle Falls, which quickly turns into a trail leading upwards; this embankment is part of the original Jasper–Banff highway.

The trailhead sign is visible on the original Banff–Jasper Highway at the left in the photo.

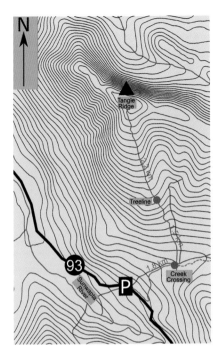

Follow the embankment for 400 m before a well-defined trail leads into the forest.

2. In the forest the trail climbs quickly, first passing an excellent viewpoint towards Mount Kitchener and Stutfield Peak before plunging into denser forest. Within 600 m the trail passes ruins of an old out-fitter cabin. Once Tangle Creek comes into view, keep an eye out for a flagged trail crossing Tangle Creek (shown below).

3. On the north side of Tangle Creek the trail can be less distinct for the first 300 m (watch for rock cairns and flagging tape). From the creek it is 1.5 km and 350 vertical metres to reach treeline. Don't forget to look behind you at the increasingly incredible views!

4. Above treeline the trail becomes faint, but navigation is straightforward. Head up the gentle scree slope, aiming for the left side of the wide summit ridge. It is 2.2 km and 600 vertical metres from treeline to the summit, so be prepared to take some time!

▼ *The trail crosses Tangle Creek at this flagged junction. In early summer, stream-crossing shoes can be advantageous.*

5. Be extremely wary of cornices and lingering snowpatches along the ridgecrest. While the true summit of Tangle Ridge is occupied by a Parks Canada radio repeater, there are still excellent views in all directions and it is possible to walk along the ridgecrest for different perspectives. When you have finished enjoying the fine summit views, retrace your steps back down the trail.

The start of the trail (centre) can be faint in places, but rock cairns and flagging tape mark the way.

Higher up the valley there are great views looking back towards Wilcox Pass (left) and Mount Andromeda (right) in the background.

As the trail ascends above treeline the trail fades.

◄ Scree makes for slow but steady progress off-trail for the last 300 vertical metres to reach the summit. Occasional rock cairns mark the most efficient route.

▲ Rather than a traditional summit cairn, the true summit of Tangle Ridge is host to a Parks Canada radio repeater. Note that this building is locked and is not a public shelter.

▼ Wide-reaching views south from the summit towards peaks around the Columbia Icefield.

3 Big Bend Campsite

A favourite for locals and visitors alike, the Chaba trail (which was until recently called Fortress Lake Trail) to Big Bend is a straightforward stroll with excellent views of Dragon Peak and mountains up the Chaba River valley. This route is also popular with mountain bikers. Note that sections of it are known to be quite muddy during the spring and after periods of substantial rainfall.

DISTANCE: 13.5 KM

HEIGHT GAIN: 250 METRES

HIGH POINT: 1400 METRES

MODERATE

MID-MAY TO MID-OCTOBER

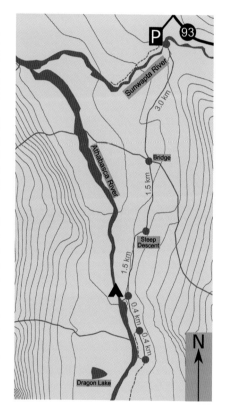

Start: From the Junction of Hwys 16 and 93 near Jasper, travel south for 53 km. Turn off the highway onto the road beside the Sunwapta Falls resort. At the end of this road is a parking area with one-way traffic in effect.

Difficulty: A pleasant, wide trail through lovely forest with minimal elevation gain. Expect muddy patches, especially in the early season. During the winter this trail is popular with cross-country skiers and snowshoers.

1. From the trailhead kiosk, descend stairs and a paved ramp towards the bridge perched above the thunderous roar of Sunwapta Falls. Cross the bridge and clamber up a short rocky step before following the wide trail that wanders into the forest. There are initially some mountain views through the forest, but as the trail moves away from the roar of the falls, the canopy thickens and views dwindle.

2. Some 1.5 km along the trail there is a perennially muddy section. The former "corduroy road" (made of wooden planks)

has melded into the marshy surface of the trail here, and you'll need careful footwork to keep your boots dry. Thankfully the muddy travel is short lived and soon the trail returns to a gentle stroll through the forest.

The trail starts by crossing the sturdy bridge over Sunwapta Falls.

3. After crossing a small bridge just past the km 3 trail marker, travel mellows and more flowers can be seen dotting the fringes of the path. The trail then rounds a short, steep descent where views of a peak unofficially named "Komodo Dragon" rises above.

4. The trail continues descending with small undulations until it reaches the km 6 trail marker. Soon after, the Athabasca River is directly in view and a junction is reached. Turn right, towards the Big Bend campground, where a short trail skirts the edge of a placid pond before reaching the campground's picnic tables with their lovely view. Be sure to wander down to the riverbank for a fine view to the north.

5. When you have finished lunch and snapped enough pictures, it is worthwhile continuing 700 m down Chaba Trail (towards the Athabasca Crossing campground), where a well-defined but unsigned spur trail traverses above the Athabasca River with good views. It is a much longer trek to reach the Athabasca Crossing campground itself (15.8 km round trip!), and it is recommended to turn around here and retrace your steps back to the parking area.

Parks Canada has worked for decades to improve muddy parts of the trail, such as this section of corduroy (boardwalk) from the 1980s that has slowly sunk into the ground.

Small creek crossings along the trail are spanned with both pedestrian and bike bridges.

Moist areas around creeks along the trail are great, lush places to see flowers like paintbrush.

▲ *Epic views looking south from the picnic tables at the Big Bend towards Fortress Lake. Mount Confederation (centre), Mount Quincy (centre right), and Dragon Peak (far right) can be seen.*

▼ *Looking up towards Dragon Peak, the trail towards Athabasca Crossing continues to the left.*

▲ Looking north along the Athabasca River from the Big Bend campsite. Peaks of Endless Chain Ridge are visible in the distance (centre).

▼ The spur trail 700 m farther down the trail towards Athabasca Crossing has impressive views of the peaks above Fortress Lake and of the meandering Athabasca River.

4 Maligne Pass

One of the most spectacular passes in Jasper National Park, Maligne has grown in popularity over the past few years with increasing traffic along this section of the Great Divide trail. Reaching the pass is a long day, and there are often damaged bridges necessitating creek crossings. Stream-crossing shoes can be beneficial to avoid rambling in soggy boots. Wait for a drier period later in the summer for this route. Dogs are not allowed on this trail, but bikes are permitted up to the Maligne Pass junction.

DISTANCE: 29 KM

HEIGHT GAIN: 900 METRES

HIGH POINT: 2250 METRES

STRENUOUS

LATE JULY TO END OF SEPTEMBER. This is avalanche terrain in the spring, and the trail is also closed during the winter for caribou conservation (check with Parks Canada for any current closures).

Start: Poboktan Creek trailhead. From the junction of Hwys 93 and 16 near Jasper, travel south on Hwy 93 for 71 km. Turn left into the signed parking area on the south side of Poboktan Creek (just after the warden station).

Difficulty: Straightforward, mellow trail with some muddy patches to reach the Maligne Pass junction. From the junction you'll encounter moderately steep, rooted trail with unbridged creek crossings and moist wetland crossings.

1. From the parking area, hike back down to the highway and cross the bridge, wandering toward the Poboktan warden station. A trailhead kiosk can be seen to the right of the station complex, with the trail starting just behind a horse stable.

2. The first stretch of trail is pleasant, gentle walking alongside Poboktan Creek before rising, with some undulations. After 4 km of travel from the road, the trail returns to Poboktan Creek, to a viewpoint with nice mountain views.

3. After the viewpoint, the trail ascends, passing over three short bridges before descending to reach the Maligne Pass junction. At the junction, turn left (heading upwards), following signage for Maligne Pass and the Avalanche campground.

4. The Maligne Pass trail is rougher and narrower than the Poboktan Creek route. Any (or perhaps all) of the bridges referenced here may be damaged or gone altogether; check with Parks Canada before setting off. At 200 m from the junction the first bridge over Poligne Creek is reached and the trail climbs steeply once you're on the other side. Over the next 3.5 km the trail continues to climb, crossing five more bridges before reaching a deeper crossing with a well-worn side trail (see picture below, do not follow the spur trail going to the left). From this crossing the trail continues to climb into more-open, pleasant forest, crossing the bridged creek to reach the Avalanche campground in 1 km.

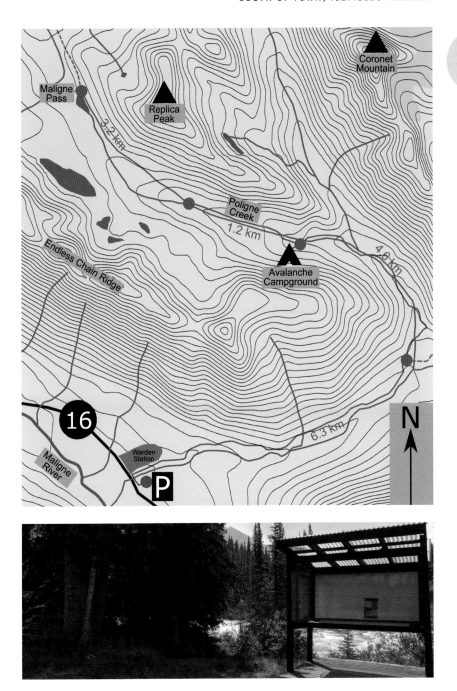

The labels on the map read:

Coronet
Mountain

Maligne
Pass

Replica
Peak

3.2 km

Poligne
Creek

1.2 km

4.6 km

Endless Chain Ridge

Avalanche
Campground

6.3 km

N

16

Warden
Station

Maligne
River

P

The unassuming start to the Poboktan Creek trail. Be sure to check the trailhead kiosk, as bear restrictions or closures are common on this route.

▲ The only bench between the trailhead and the Avalanche campground 800 m along the trail. This is a great spot to stop and admire the flowing waters of Poboktan Creek on the return trip.

▼ There are few viewpoints along the trail before reaching the Maligne Pass junction, but peaks of the Winston Churchill range can be seen from here alongside Poboktan Creek.

After the Maligne Pass junction, the trail narrows and the number of flowers increases (including columbine as seen here).

Some of the creek crossings can be quite difficult in high water. Be prepared to turn around if a stream is too deep or its current too swift. The trail continues on the other side of the creek. Do not be tempted by the spur trail to the left.

5. The Avalanche campground is a great place for a break, and for a shorter day it is a worthwhile objective by itself (it is just over 11 km back to the trailhead from here). Leaving the campground, the trail passes through a creekside wetland for 1 km before a final crossing of Poligne Creek (look for orange flagging tape along indistinct sections). Once on the north side of the creek, the trail ascends on good trail with short bushy sections. Views continue to open up as the trail works its way higher, and after 1 km, panoramic views across the valley can be seen.

6. Carry on a further 1.5 km on a gentle, well-defined trail to reach a pristine sapphire lake that marks the watershed of Maligne Pass. Be sure to stay on the defined trail, as this is an environmentally sensitive area. When you have finished snapping pictures from the pass, retrace your steps back to the road.

Higher up the trail, mountain views improve and the terrain becomes more rugged.

FROM TOP: *After the Avalanche campground, the trail passes through moist but scenic wetland before reaching the alpine; Some of the most spectacular terrain in the park can be seen along the way to Maligne Pass. To the left are peaks of Endless Chain Ridge; A pretty lake marks the summit of Maligne Pass. The trail continues to the right, gradually descending into forest. Backpackers can continue on a multi-day trek which eventually reaches the facilities on the north shore of Maligne Lake (a lengthy 34 km and one deep river crossing away).*

5 Second Geraldine Lake

Lakes, waterfalls and mountain views await those who would wander up the Geraldine valley. Travel to the first lake is quite straightforward, though often muddy. Carrying on to reach the second lake is more involved but does have fantastic viewpoints. Neither bikes nor horses nor dogs are allowed on this trail.

In 2023 Parks Canada started construction of a woodland caribou captive breeding facility near this trail. Check with the Jasper National Park trail office before setting off, to confirm whether the access road is open to public traffic.

DISTANCE: 10.5 KM (TO SECOND GERALDINE LAKE)

HEIGHT GAIN: 500 METRES (TO SECOND GERALDINE LAKE)

HIGH POINT: 1910 METRES

STRENUOUS

LATE JULY TO END OF SEPTEMBER. NOT ADVISABLE DURING OR AFTER SUSTAINED RAINFALL.

Start: Geraldine Lakes trailhead. From the junction of Hwys 93 and 16 near Jasper, travel south on Hwy 93 for 30 km and turn right onto Hwy 93A, following signage for Athabasca Falls. Drive past the Athabasca Falls parking area, cross the Athabasca River and turn left onto the next signed junction for Geraldine Road. Geraldine Road is quite rough and a four-wheel-drive high-clearance vehicle is recommended (alternatively, park in the pullout at the start of Geraldine Road and travel on bikes to reach the trailhead). Drive for 5.4 km (gaining 300 vertical metres) to reach the Geraldine Lakes trailhead. Geraldine Road is closed seasonally from November until early May.

Difficulty: A challenging trail that can be steep in places, with sustained patches of mud and roots. As described above, wait

Before reaching First Geraldine Lake there are many muddy patches of trail.

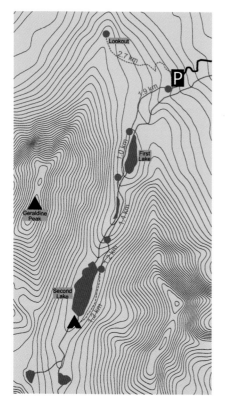

During warm periods in early summer, parts of the trail can often be flooded as shown here, where bypass trails (out of view to the right) have been worn into the forest.

footwork is required, especially when wet. The trail then follows directly beside the outflow of First Geraldine Lake. Spur trails have been formed in the bush on the right of the trail to allow passage during high water. About 200 m after the creek crossing, a signed viewpoint for First Geraldine Lake is reached.

3. The trail then follows the lakeshore for 800 m before crossing a rockslide (look for yellow diamonds and pink flagging tape), working towards the inflow of the lake. A steep, rooted and rocky climb then gains 50 vertical metres before coming to an unmarked junction. Head left for a short diversion to a viewpoint overlooking the first lake or stay straight for the main trail. At the top of the slope, scurry across boulders, following cairns and yellow diamonds over the next 300 m before a pretty puddle comes into view, with Geraldine Falls looming in the background.

4. Following along the shore of the puddle, which can seem like a proper lake during high water, the trail hops across rocks before passing through a section of forest and emerging on a well-defined, rocky track to reach a sign near the base of Geraldine Falls. A small spur trail on the right leads to a great viewpoint of the falls while the main trail heads steeply upwards, weaving

until later in the season when water levels are lower to avoid sections of flooded trail. Between the first and the second lakes there are sections of boulder-hopping and steep scree that toe the boundary between difficult hiking and easy scrambling.

1. The wide but very rooty trail leaves the parking area and travels through peaceful pine forest, soon gaining elevation. The first 1.2 km is perennially muddy (watch your footing, as some places can be way more than boot deep!) and showcases the various mud-mitigation methods that have been tried across the decades. After passing several old, rotten bridges, the trail flattens and the mud subsides.

2. The trail then descends towards First Geraldine Lake. Just before the lake comes into view, the descent steepens and careful

▲ First Geraldine Lake is a pristine mountain paradise. "Fluted Peak" rises across the lake as the trail follows the lakeshore.

► When passing through rockslides, the trail is marked by yellow diamonds (highlighted here with a red dot) or rock cairns.

▼ The trail hops across boulders on the left shore of this puddle between First and Second Geraldine lakes.

▲ *Geraldine Falls thunders beside you as the trail works its way up a steep scree slope to Second Geraldine Lake.*

▼ *Excellent views down towards First Geraldine Lake, with peaks of Endless Chain Ridge visible in the distance.*

a path through scree to ascend the slope left of the waterfall (look for yellow diamonds).

5. Working up the steep scree here can be quite a grunt. Be careful if there are hikers above who could dislodge rocks down on you. After gaining 150 vertical metres, the trail darts into the bush, descending briefly to a nice break spot before clambering over one last section of boulders where Second Geraldine Lake comes into view.

6. The described route ends here, but for a longer day it is possible to continue among boulders on the east shore of the lake, following cairns and yellow diamonds, to reach the Geraldine Lakes campground. Retrace your steps back to the trailhead, being careful when descending the steep scree slopes.

There are spectacular views all around Second Geraldine Lake. For a longer day, it is possible to carry on above the left shore to the campground at the south end of the lake.

Going farther: Geraldine Fire Lookout

You may have wondered why there is a road leading up to the trailhead in the first place. Historically, the Geraldine road was an access route for the Geraldine fire lookout. While the lookout itself has been removed, there is a still a good view of the Whirlpool River valley and Mount Kerkeslin to be had from the top. The old road can be bushy in places but travel is straightforward.

Although the old road is well defined, it can be quite bushy in places.

DISTANCE: 5.4 KM

HEIGHT GAIN: 250 METRES

HIGH POINT: 1710 METRES

From the Geraldine Lakes trailhead, the route follows the old road (now barricaded to vehicles by concrete blocks) leaving the northwest part of the parking area. Follow the old road upwards as it ascends, with several bushy sections to be battled through.

1. At 2.7 km from parking, the trail flattens and the small plateau where the lookout tower used to stand is reached. To look down into the Whirlpool Valley, continue forward, edging down on a bare section of rock The viewpoint for Mount Kerkeslin can be seen on the right.

2. Retrace your steps back to the parking area.

Along the lookout road you'll see many whitebark pines. This is an endangered species, so be sure to give these trees some space.

The old lookout gives an impressive view across the Whirlpool River valley, home to the Athabasca Pass trail.

6 Cavell Meadows and Path of the Glacier Trail

With a trailhead elevation of 1770 metres, the Cavell Meadows route is one of the easiest ways to hike in the alpine in Jasper National Park. Excellent views of Mount Edith Cavell and Angel Glacier, vast wildflower-filled slopes and encounters with alpine wildlife such as hoary marmots await those who meander up these meadows. Neither dogs nor bikes are allowed on the Cavell Meadows trail.

DISTANCE: 8 KM

HEIGHT GAIN: 525 METRES

HIGH POINT: 2300 METRES

MODERATE

LATE JUNE TO END OF SEPTEMBER. The Cavell Meadows trail, its surrounding area and its access road are subject to an area closure during the winter months, for caribou conservation.

Start: From the junction of Hwys 93 and 16 near Jasper, travel south on Hwy 93 for 7 km and then turn right onto Hwy 93A, following signage for Wabasso Road. Continue along Hwy 93A for just over 5 km before turning right onto Cavell Road. Drive up Cavell for 14 km to the trailhead and parking area at the end of the road. Cavell Road is closed from late October until early June.

Difficulty: A wide and easy to follow trail that is steep and muddy in places. Reaching

Crossing over Cavell Creek, with Mount Edith Cavell looming above. The East Ridge (left skyline ridge) is a popular technical alpine climbing route.

the upper viewpoint requires some travel on steep scree (proper hiking footwear strongly recommended). Snow patches can linger here until mid-July.

1. From the parking area, head up towards Mount Edith Cavell. Stay left on a broad, paved trail with increasingly impressive views up towards the peak as the route gains elevation.

2. It is worthwhile to visit the Path of the Glacier viewpoint first before heading up to the meadows. Carry on up the well-graded trail for 300 m, passing by the Cavell

Meadows junction to reach the viewpoint. Respect the signage around the viewpoint and do not descend to Cavell Glacier Lake, due to flash flooding danger.

3. Backtrack 150 m to the Cavell Meadows junction and start heading up the rougher, rocky trail. Over the next 1 km, the path works its way steadily upwards, following the side of the moraine, before it reaches an excellent viewpoint and then enters the forest.

4. The trail climbs, steeply in places, for the next 600 m before reaching the Cavell

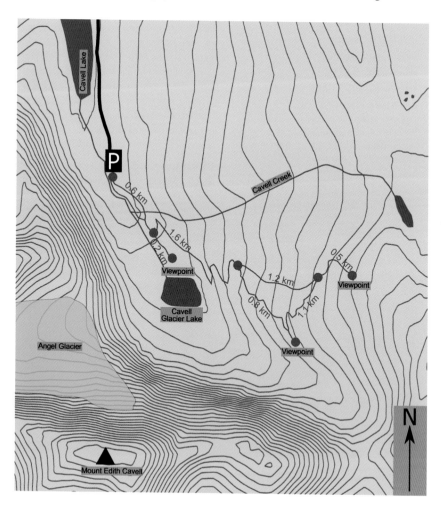

Meadows loop junction. It is recommended to head left at the junction (going up the steeper path) and return on the mellower trail.

5. Excellent views and the piercing whistle of marmots await hikers as they work upwards. Stay left at a junction with a connector trail. Over the next 900 m, the trail

▲ *The first part of the Cavell Meadows route overlaps with the partly paved Path of the Glacier trail.*

▼ *In 2012 Ghost Glacier fell off Mount Edith Cavell into Cavell Glacier Lake, causing a flash flood that ravaged the landscape and parking area below. Angel Glacier (right) has been rapidly receding each summer since 2012. Parks has strongly cautioned hikers against descending to the lake in case another flash flood occurs.*

Picturesque meadows, nearby glaciers and the classic call of hoary marmots make Cavell Meadows a must-visit destination.

▲ *The outlier peak of Mount Edith Cavell is locally known as Mount Sorrow (centre).*

climbs steeply before reaching the first viewpoint junction.

6. To reach the first junction, the high point of the trail, ascend steadily over the next 500 m on dirt and scree, gaining 100 vertical metres to a cairn and viewpoint. Spur trails keep climbing higher up the ridgecrest but are not recommended. Return the way you came, back to the previous junction.

7. To reach the next viewpoint, a connector trail works towards the peak for 700 m, with yellow diamonds marking several indistinct sections. A small 100 m side trail leads to the second viewpoint, which boasts views of Cavell Glacier Lake as well as the peak itself.

8. Carry on downwards along the mellower trail to complete the loop, reaching the loop junction in 800 m. Once back in the forest, continue descending and retrace your steps back to the parking area.

▼ *Cavell Meadows is a wildflower enthusiast's dream.*

▲ The trail leading to the first (highest) viewpoint is steep in places but grants a far-reaching view.

▼ Hoary marmots are some of the main residents of Cavell Meadows. Be sure to give them space and not leave any food scraps around.

7 Whirlpool River and Moab Lake

The start of the historic Athabasca Pass Trail described here makes for a full-day hike with minimal elevation change and several great viewpoints. If planning to follow the described extension to see the remains of the historic Tie camp, it is recommended to bring bikes for the first 8.5 km of old fire road.

DISTANCE: 13.5 KM

HEIGHT GAIN: 300 METRES

HIGH POINT: 1260 METRES

EASY

LATE MAY TO END OF SEPTEMBER. The Moab Lake road is closed seasonally from November until early May.

Start: To reach the trailhead it is recommended to have a high-clearance vehicle, as the road can be quite rough. From the junction of Hwys 93 and 16 near Jasper, travel south on Hwy 93 for 7 km and turn right, onto Hwy 93A, following signage for Wabasso Road. Stay on Hwy 93A for 15 km and then turn right, onto Moab Lake Road. Carry on for just under 7 km to reach the parking area at the end of the road.

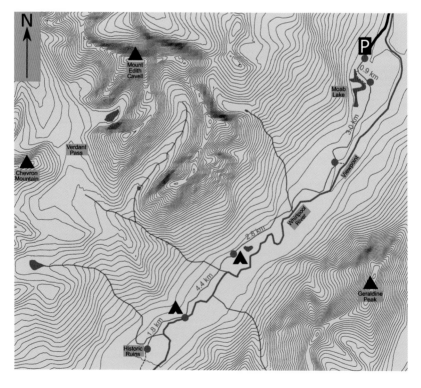

Difficulty: Straightforward travel on an old gravel road.

1. Just over 4 km along Moab Lake Road, it is worthwhile stopping at a riverside viewpoint with red chairs that grants a great view of the Whirlpool River with Geraldine Mountain looming above.

2. Before leaving the parking area, take the time to read the interpretive signage describing the history of Athabasca Pass. Also examine the map of the Whirlpool valley: it is quite the trek to get all the way to the pass!

A picnic table perched above Moab Lake makes for a great break spot.

3. Leaving the parking area, the trail is wide and travel is swift. After 400 m, the trail reaches interpretive signs describing the Moab Lake fire of July 2000 and the benefits that small-scale fires have on the landscape. It is worthwhile heading down to the shore of Moab Lake and snapping some pictures: this is a popular destination for fishing and it is common to see folks in boats out trying to reel in dinner. There is a rugged trail that follows the lakeshore and links up with the main route, but it is often bushy and covered in deadfall. Retrace your steps back to the junction and carry on along the main trail.

The small hills along the trail allow for distant views farther up the Whirlpool River valley. Geraldine Peak is visible on the left.

4. Some 500 m farther along, a picnic table overlooking Moab Lake grants a great view of the Whirlpool River valley and peaks above. Carry on along the gentle road. A section of denser forest just past the km 3 distance marker offers a good break spot and a reprieve from the sun.

5. Descending from the break spot, the trail bends east and a well-defined spur trail can be seen leading down to the river. This spur can be a good viewpoint looking up towards Geraldine Peak and is used by rafters and kayakers floating down the Whirlpool River.

Regrowth in the trailside forest burned in the 2000 Moab Lake fire shows the regenerative effects of fire on the landscape.

6. Past the spur trail, it is 2.8 km over a few small hills and past a lovely trailside pond to reach the Whirlpool campground. Historically, the public was able to drive right to this spot, and just past the junction a small pullout on the north side of the trail used to serve as a parking area. There are great views to be had from the campground, and it is a fine place for a picnic or quick break if continuing. If you decide not to do the extension described below, retrace your steps back along the road.

The short spur trail to a riverside viewpoint can be bushy in places but is still a worthwhile wander.

Near the Whirlpool campground, the forest opens and there are more impressive views up towards Geraldine Peak to be enjoyed.

Lovely views looking south up the Whirlpool River from the Whirlpool campground.

Going farther: Historic Tie Camp

If time and energy permit, there are additional excellent mountain views and historic fur-trade-era relics to be seen farther along the Athabasca Pass trail.

DISTANCE: ADD 12 KM (FROM THE
WHIRLPOOL CAMPGROUND AND BACK)

HEIGHT GAIN: ADD 150 METRES

HIGH POINT: 1270 METRES

The end of the old fire road is well marked with both historical and recent signage.

1. After leaving the Whirlpool campground, keep following the old road for 2.0 km, then turn right, onto the signed trail to Tie Camp.

2. The trail travels across two unbridged creeks and through rolling verdant forest to reach the Tie campground. Leaving the Tie campground, the route crosses a muddy wetland for 200 m before travelling directly

Creek crossings along the Athabasca Pass trail can be quite deep after periods of heavy rainfall and in the spring.

beside the Whirlpool River amidst lovely mountain views. The riverside viewpoint is a great destination by itself, and if time is short, consider turning back here.

3. Over the next 1.5 km the trail undulates and moves back into the forest before reaching an unbridged creek crossing. Some 250 m past the creek the trail crosses the remains of the Tie camp, including portions of several historical cabins, a wagon wheel and various artifacts. Do not touch the relics, as they can be quite fragile.

An excellent viewpoint towards Needle Peak (right) and Mount Kane (left) just after the muddy meadow guarding the Tie Camp campground.

Various historical relics, including the wagon wheel shown here and several ruined cabins, mark the original Tie Camp.

8 Astoria River to Switchback Viewpoint

While the Tonquin Valley is mostly the domain of backpackers, strong hikers can travel swiftly along the Astoria River to experience this part of the valley and be surrounded by its great views. For a shorter day, consider stopping at the pretty break spot on the Astoria River at 8.6 km along the trail. Neither dogs nor bikes are allowed on this trail.

DISTANCE: 27 KM

HEIGHT GAIN: 550 METRES

HIGH POINT: 2110 METRES

MODERATE

EARLY JULY TO END OF SEPTEMBER. The Tonquin Valley and its access road are subject to an area closure during the winter months, for caribou conservation.

Start: From the junction of Hwys 93 and 16 near Jasper, travel south on Hwy 93 for 7 km and then turn right, onto Hwy 93A, following signage for Wabasso Road. Continue along Hwy 93A for just over 5 km before turning right, onto Cavell Road. Drive up Cavell Road for 14 km: the trailhead and parking are just past the second signed viewpoint. Cavell Road is subject to a seasonal closure from late October until early June.

Difficulty: Good travel on a well-maintained but often moist trail. Expect several small stream crossings and one rubbly patch crossing a rockslide.

1. From the parking area, the trail gently descends to a wide bridge spanning Cavell Creek. In clear weather the view up towards Mount Edith Cavell from the bridge is an awesome sight to behold. Having crossed the bridge, the trail ascends and comes to a signed junction. Stay right for the hiker trail; left goes to a staging area for horses. After a few initial undulations the route settles into a steady traverse high above the Astoria River.

▲ The trail starts by crossing over Cavell Creek, with excellent views up towards Mount Edith Cavell.

▼ An impressive view of Throne Mountain from the Astoria River bridge.

2. For the next 1.5 km, the trail works deeper into the Tonquin Valley on mostly flat gravel, crossing several short bridges. The route then descends gently with a few shallow seasonal stream crossings before arriving at a bridge over Verdant Creek.

3. Once across Verdant Creek, the trail continues to descend and in 300 m crosses over the roaring Astoria River. The cacophony is short-lived, however, as the trail then rises into dense and much quieter forest with a few short bridges to bypass muddy sections.

4. After passing the Astoria campground, the trail undulates above the river, with several perennially soggy sections, before reaching a signed junction. Stay straight on trail 105; left leads to Chrome Lake and the Alpine Club of Canada's Wates-Gibson Hut via a much rougher route. Some 80 m farther there is a great break spot, maintained by horse parties, that has sturdy benches

and an outhouse. For a shorter day, this spot is a worthwhile destination by itself.

5. From the break spot it is just under 5 km and 380 vertical metres to the scenic Switchback campground and viewpoint. The trail rises gently at first, on rocky terrain, before reaching the edge of a signed danger zone, some 300 m wide, which is prone to rockfall, particularly during rainy periods. Hikers should move through this zone as quickly as possible.

▲ *Much of the trail to the Astoria campground has tranquil mountain views such as this one of Mount Sorrow.*

▼ *Stay right at the well-signed Chrome Lake trail junction.*

6. Once back in the forest, the trail ascends switchbacks (hence the campground's name). As the gentle but steady grade weaves upwards, the vegetation gradually changes from lower subalpine forest into treeline meadows. When the trail loops back along the rockfall, there are fine views across the valley towards Throne Mountain and Blackhorn Peak.

7. Atop the switchbacks, the trail mellows and there are impressive views towards the glaciated peaks of The Ramparts. At the Switchback campground junction it is 100 (often muddy) metres off the main trail to reach the campground, which makes a nice spot for a break.

8. Retrace your steps back down to the road, making sure to travel quickly through the rockslide zone.

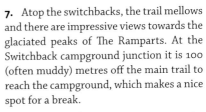

▲ This "hitching rail" break area is a great viewpoint and a lovely place to turn around for a shorter day. Thunderbolt Peak (centre) and its unnamed outlier (left of centre) are visible in the distance.

▲ There are many trailside viewpoints along the sustained switchbacks. The summit glacier on Campus Peak (left) is visible in the distance.

▼ Atop the switchbacks the forest opens to great views. Rising above the trail on the left is Oldhorn Mountain.

▼ The meadow before the Switchback campground has excellent views of glaciated peaks among The Ramparts, the iconic mountain range of the Tonquin Valley.

9 Maccarib Pass

Following the course of Portal Creek, a day hike to Maccarib Pass travels through spectacular treeline and alpine terrain with wide-reaching views. For a shorter day, hiking along the trail to an open talus slope 6 km from the parking area also gives great mountain views. Neither dogs nor bikes are allowed on this trail.

DISTANCE: 26 KM

HEIGHT GAIN: 750 METRES

HIGH POINT: 2210 METRES

MODERATE

EARLY JULY TO END OF SEPTEMBER. The Tonquin Valley, and access road are subject to an area closure for caribou conservation during the winter months.

Start: From the junction of Hwys 93 and 16 near Jasper, travel south of Hwy 93 for 7 km and then turn right onto Hwy 93A, following signage for Wabasso Road. Travel up Hwy 93A for 2.5 km and then turn right, onto Marmot Road. Continue climbing on Marmot Road for 6.5 km and then turn left into the Portal Creek/Tonquin Valley parking area just before the bridge over Portal Creek.

Difficulty: Expect a mixture of trail conditions including muddy patches, rubbly sections, and deep ruts. Early in the summer or after periods of high rainfall, sections of the trail near Portal Creek are often flooded. Snow patches can linger near Maccarib Pass until mid-July.

1. The trail starts on the south side of Portal Creek and meanders on rock and roots for 300 m before crossing the creek. As the trail ascends the valley it passes through several muddy sections and open traverses that give views up The Portal (as this valley is called, also lending its name to Portal Creek, including towards Peveril and Lectern peaks.

2. Some 4 km from the parking area, the trail crosses a wide bridge over Circus Creek, and after a short, steep climb it emerges from the forest to traverse open

◄ *The trail crosses Portal Creek over a sturdy bridge soon after the trailhead.*

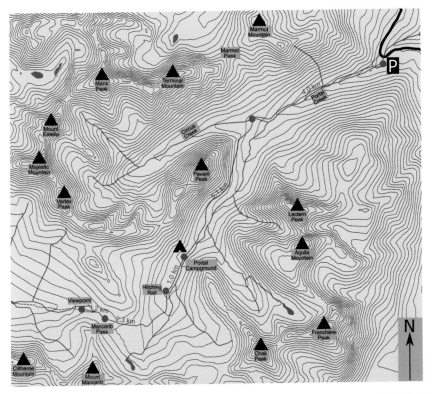

When the trail leaves the forest, there are great views to be seen, including this one towards Lectern Peak.

45

▲ *Peveril Peak looms above as the trail crosses over Circus Creek.*

▼ *There are many photo opportunities as the trail traverses several rockslides.*

talus slopes below Peveril Peak. For a short day, these open slopes offer impressive mountain views and are a worthwhile trek by themselves. After 1 km in the open, the trail briefly returns to the forest for a welcome bit of shade. When it emerges again there are far-reaching views towards Oldhorn Mountain and Mount Maccarib.

3. The trail then gradually descends to the bank of Portal Creek. The terrain by the creek is still reasonably open, with fine views towards Chak Peak and Aquila Mountain. The trail braids in several places, and in high water the main (creek-adjacent) branches can often be flooded.

4. The trail continues to follow Portal Creek for just over 1 km before reaching the Portal Creek campground. After the campground, three bridges draw the trail back and forth across the creek before passing by a horse staging area, complete with

▲ *The Tonquin Valley is known for being muddy, and some soggy sections are unavoidable.*

▼ *Looking down The Portal valley towards the trailhead after reaching treeline.*

hitching rail, benches and an outhouse, that makes a good spot for a break.

5. The trail works upwards towards Maccarib Pass on eroded rock and dirt, but excellent views in all directions make for a very pleasant stroll. The official Parks Canada sign for Maccarib Pass (elevation 2210 metres) is a nice viewpoint, but I strongly recommend continuing a further 1.2 km (descending about 50 metres of elevation), when peaks of The Ramparts can first be seen.

6. When you have finished admiring the alpine scenery, return the way you came, back towards the parking area.

▲ *Many mountains, including Chak Peak (centre) and Mount Edith Cavell (right of centre) can be seen from the Maccarib Pass sign.*

▼ *It is very worthwhile to carry on down the trail to see part of The Ramparts, the iconic mountain range of the Tonquin Valley.*

10 The Whistlers

Well known as the destination of the Jasper SkyTram, the summit of The Whistlers can also be accessed via a steep but rewarding hiking trail. In late 2020 Jasper SkyTram announced significant future renovations that will relocate both the upper and the lower terminals. Check with Jasper SkyTram for current details. As of 2023, one-way tickets were available to save your knees some strain on the way down!

DISTANCE: 15.4 KM

HEIGHT GAIN: 1200 METRES

HIGH POINT: 2460 METRES

STRENUOUS

EARLY JULY TO END OF SEPTEMBER. Avalanche terrain is encountered in the upper portion of the trail, and travel is not recommended until the route is free of snow (confirm with the Parks Canada trail office before setting off). Whistlers Trail is subject to an area closure during the winter months, for caribou conservation.

Start: Parking Area 14. From the junction of Hwys 93 and 16 near Jasper, travel south on Hwy 93 for 1.8 km and turn right, onto Whistlers Road. Drive 2.7 km on Whistlers before turning left onto a signed gravel side road.

Difficulty: A steep and sustained trail that can be quite rooted. A signed detour through a rockslide requires difficult footwork and can be treacherous when wet.

1. From the parking area, the trail starts climbing through lush montane forest. In 400 m, stay on the main trail (following signage for trail 5) where a junction with trail 5b (the evocatively named mountain bike trail Swamp Rider) is encountered. This section of forest is dense with flowers such as common harebell, columbine and paintbrush.

2. After 1 km, the trail starts to steepen. Roots and rocky steps are encountered as short switchbacks make quick work of elevation. Thankfully, the grade mellows 2 km from the trailhead, and the route passes through a boulder field via a signed detour.

3. Look for yellow diamonds and pink flagging tape on the far (west) side of the boulder field. Footing can be somewhat tricky at times, and be extra cautious if surfaces

◀ *The start of The Whistlers trail can seem like quite a jungle, but the path is easy to follow.*

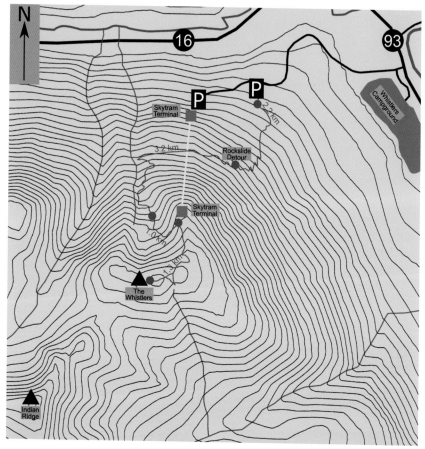

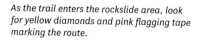

As the trail enters the rockslide area, look for yellow diamonds and pink flagging tape marking the route.

Travel along the detour can be quite slow and requires careful footwork.

▲ After you've passed under the SkyTram, the forest starts to thin and you'll get glimpses of mountains in the Victoria Cross Ranges across the valley.

▼ The last stretch of the trail before reaching the ridgecrest can be steep and rocky, but excellent views more than make up for it.

are wet. The signed detour ascends on the edge of the forest before passing west into two further sections of boulders before returning into the trees on a more conventional hiking trail.

4. After leaving the boulder field, the trail starts a rising traverse wrapping around the mountain and passing underneath the SkyTram line. The trail then switchbacks higher as it nears treeline, and there are views across the valley towards the Victoria Cross Ranges. As the forest thins, keep your eyes open for yellow diamond trail markers that point the least steep way to ascend into the alpine.

5. It is a steep climb to gain the last 200 metres of elevation from treeline to the SkyTram junction, but impressive views towards Pyramid Mountain and the Pyramid Bench give great excuses for numerous breaks.

6. After 6.5 km and 1000 metres of elevation gain from the parking area, the trail joins with the SkyTram-accessed Whistlers Summit route. It is a further 1.2 km and 200 metres of elevation to reach the summit, travelling up a steady climb on a well-marked and bordered trail complete with numerous benches. Please stay on designated trails, as this sensitive alpine area sees extensive traffic.

The upper section of The Whistlers trail can hold snow into July and is dangerous during the winter and spring due to avalanche hazard. Check with Parks Canada for current conditions before setting off in the early season.

After you pass the upper SkyTram terminal, the grade mellows and a very well-defined trail leads to the summit.

The Whistlers is situated for a perfect summit panorama of the Athabasca Valley and peaks as distant as the mighty Mount Robson.

11 Curator Lake via Wabasso Lake

A lengthy day trip to one of the most scenic parts of Jasper's famous Skyline Trail. This route offers a way to experience the area around Curator Lake and Big Shovel Pass that does not rely on securing a site at the very popular Curator campground.

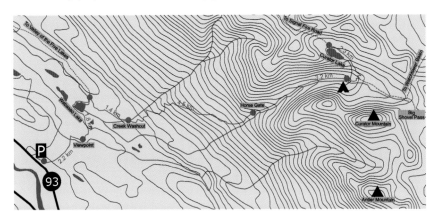

DISTANCE: 31 KM

HEIGHT GAIN: 1200 METRES

HIGH POINT: 2300 METRES

STRENUOUS

EARLY JULY TO END OF SEPTEMBER

Start: Parking Area 16. From the junction of Hwys 93 and 16 near Jasper, travel south on Hwy 93 for 14 km and turn left into Parking Area 16, following signage for Wabasso Lake.

Difficulty: Consistent travel on fair trail. Expect some muddy and overgrown sections in the latter half of the trail, as well as several unbridged creek crossings.

1. Leaving the parking area, the trail first parallels the road before undulating over several small ridges to reach a fine lookout over the Athabasca valley. From here it is just under 1 km to Wabasso Lake, with its own well-trodden viewpoint allowing access down to the lake. The trail traverses around the lakeshore over the next 600 m, passing several more viewpoints before returning into the forest.

2. The trail descends to reach a hiker/horse junction. Stay right, on the hiker trail, crossing an unnamed creek before reaching the trail 9/trail 101 junction. Turn right, onto trail 101. The route soon crosses an unbridged shallow creek before gradually gaining elevation in a beautiful aspen forest. After 1.25 km you'll come to an unsigned junction. Stay on flat terrain, following directly beside the creek before reaching an open gravel flat (see image below). Yellow markers lead to an open rocky stretch with good views back towards the Trident Range. After a series of rocky switchbacks, the trail moves into the forest. Be forewarned: the next good viewpoint will be a lengthy 5 km and 700 vertical metres away.

3. In the forest, the trail can be steep in places and the grade only increases as you work your way up. Just above 1800 metres elevation, you come to a horse gate, after which the forest changes from lodgepole pine to subalpine fir. The trail flattens and travel becomes quite pleasant for 2 km before the Shovel Pass lodge comes into view. Cross the creek and follow a well-defined

▼ *Before you reach Wabasso Lake, there are great vistas down the Athabasca Valley. Mount Hardisty (left) and Mount Kerkeslin (centre) dominate the view here.*

▼▼ *Particularly on a calm morning, there are few lakes as serene as Wabasso. This can be a great place to see waterfowl as well as larger species such as moose.*

track upwards between the first two lodge buildings to reach the Curator campground.

4. From the campground, gentle switchbacks work upwards until the trail emerges into the alpine with great views in all directions. When you reach a junction with the Skyline trail, follow signage for The Notch. Some 400 m after the junction, you'll arrive at Curator Lake. If energy allows, travelling a further 700 m towards The Notch makes for great views from a perch above Curator Lake looking towards Curator Mountain.

5. When you have finished taking pictures, work your way back to the parking area.

▼▼ *The trail becomes indistinct where it crosses a washed-out gravel flat. Trend left and look for yellow trail markers on the far side of the creek.*

▼ *After you've joined Curator Lake Trail, the forest opens and travel is pleasant.*

◄ Near the end of the forested section of the trail, flowers and heather can be found in verdant abundance.

▼ The trail passes right through the scenic grounds of Shovel Pass Lodge. Curator Mountain is visible on the left.

▼▼ Between Big Shovel Pass and Curator Lake lies some of the most scenic terrain along the famous Skyline Trail.

Overlooking Curator Lake. The infamous Notch, the crux of Skyline Trail, is the corniced snow patch on the ridge just right of centre.

12 Valley of the Five Lakes

The Valley of the Five Lakes is one of the most popular destinations in Jasper National Park. Picturesque glacial lakes and impressive nearby mountains make for lovely views. The loop described here travels to all five lakes as well as through a peaceful stretch of forest, enabling hikers to fully appreciate this immense landscape.

DISTANCE: 9.2 KM

HEIGHT GAIN: 150 METRES

HIGH POINT: 1150 METRES

EASY

EARLY JUNE TO MID-OCTOBER

Leaving the trailhead, the route is broad and mellow but serves as a good warm-up to the rest of the route.

Start: Parking Area 15. From the junction of Hwys 93 and 16 near Jasper, travel south on Hwy 93 for 9 km and turn left into Parking Area 15, following signage for Valley of the Five Lakes.

Difficulty: Good travel on one of the signature trails in Jasper National Park. Expect several short, steep hills and isolated muddy patches after periods of heavy rainfall.

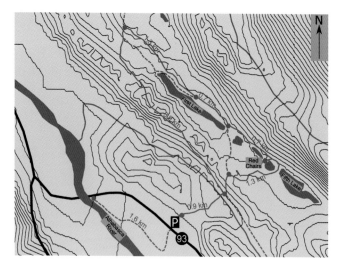

Note: *This map has a contour interval of 20 metres.*

▲ Early morning is a great time to visit the five lakes. Fourth Lake is seen here from a spur trail.

▼ Looking across the emerald waters of Fifth Lake, with Mount Hardisty in the distance.

▼▼ The red chair viewpoint between Third and Fourth lakes is a fine place to take a break and enjoy the scenery.

1. From the parking area, the wide trail leads through the forest for 800 m before crossing a narrow bridge and coming to a junction. Stay straight ahead, making your way up switchbacks on the open slope to reach the junction of trails 9a and 9b.

2. Stay to the right on trail 9a as it works its way around a pond and down a small, steep hill before crossing a stream. A steep, unsigned spur trail on the left leads down to a viewpoint on the shore of Fourth Lake. Soon after, Fifth Lake comes into view, its scenic bench and floating dock both making for great photo spots.

59

▲ The north shore of First Lake is one of the most scenic viewpoints along the Valley of the Five Lakes loop and well worth the short detour.

▼ After leaving First Lake there are still several nice overlooks beside the trail. The iconic north face of Mount Edith Cavell is visible on the right.

◄ *To complete the described loop, the route travels through pleasant forest along trail 9.*

▼ *Open grassy slopes with distant mountain views are a fine way to finish the Valley of the Five Lakes loop.*

3. Follow the trail as it skirts above the shore of Fourth Lake. It is worthwhile turning left on a signed spur trail leading to a red chair viewpoint overlooking Third Lake. Spur trails continue down to the shores of both Third and Fourth lakes. When finished snapping pictures return to the main trail, which parallels the viewpoint spurs above Third Lake and crosses a trailside viewpoint of Second Lake. At the junction of trails 9a and 9b stay straight, traversing above First Lake.

4. Carry on for 700 m above First Lake before coming to an unsigned junction branching to a lower trail. This lower trail merits the effort, as it leads to a fine viewpoint on the north shore of First Lake. Return to the main (upper) trail after the

viewpoint via a short, steep connector that is a 50 m backtrack from the north shore of First Lake.

5. There are several photogenic rock outcrops along the trail with views towards Whistlers Peak and Marmot Mountain before reaching the junction with trail 9. Turn left, heading down to a bridged bubbling brook. The trail then reascends with switchbacks before reaching an unnamed puddle and weaving through a longer stretch of enclosed forest. The trail eventually emerges above a clearing with great views of peaks to the west and south before completing the loop.

6. Turn right and cross the long, narrow bridge to return to the parking area.

MALIGNE VALLEY

13 Opal Hills Loop

A steep and scenic tour above Maligne Lake, the Opal Hills loop is an excellent option for good exercise and expansive alpine views amid copious wildflowers. Neither dogs nor bikes are allowed on this trail.

DISTANCE: 7.5 KM

HEIGHT GAIN: 500 METRES

HIGH POINT: 2230 METRES

STRENUOUS

LATE JUNE TO THE END OF SEPTEMBER. This area is often subject to closures or restrictions in July and August due to grizzly bear activity.

Start: From the junction of Hwys 93 and 16 near Jasper, travel east on Hwy 16 for 6 km before turning right onto Maligne Road and crossing the Athabasca River. Stay on Maligne Road, following signage for Maligne Lake for 43 km, before turning left into a signed parking area. Having entered the first parking area, turn left and drive to an upper parking lot, where the trailhead kiosk is visible.

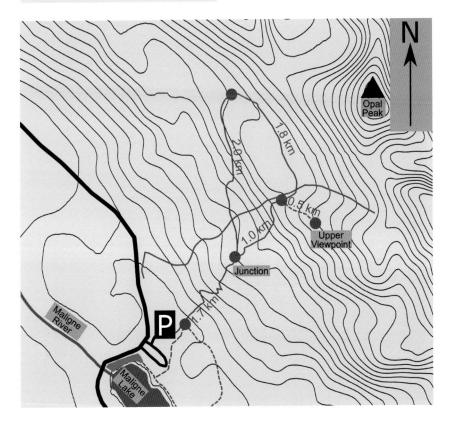

► *The well-signed start of the trail is a good warm-up before the steep elevation gain starts.*

▼ *While the trail is steep and sustained, there are many switchbacks and meanders to help lessen the grade.*

▼▼ *Hard work to reach treeline pays off with excellent views across the valley to mountains of the Maligne Range.*

Difficulty: Steep and sustained, this trail will be sure to warm you up during the ascent! Expect rooted sections, with muddy patches early in the season or after heavy rainfall.

1. The trail begins on the northeast side of the parking area, travelling over many roots that can be quite slippery when wet. Stay left at the junction with Mary Schäffer Loop and cross the clearing. From here the trail starts to climb.

2. It is just over 400 vertical metres from trailhead to treeline, and this route gobbles up that elevation quickly. There are a few short mellow sections where you can catch your breath, but overall the trail heads steeply upward over the next 1.3 km before reaching a signed junction. At the junction, it is recommended to turn right, to ascend

▼ *The described spur trails leads to this wonderful viewpoint overlooking the northern half of Maligne Lake.*

▼▼ *The Opal Hills loop winds its way through the meadow at the left of the photo. Opal Peak rises majestically on the right.*

the steeper path first and then return by the mellower trail.

3. After the junction there is still 150 vertical metres to climb on steep, forested switchbacks which flow into a steadily rising traverse. After reaching treeline, the main trail turns left while a well-trodden spur trail cuts to the right, leading up into sparse forest. If time and energy permit, it is worthwhile to follow the spur trail for 400 m to a great viewpoint overlooking Maligne Lake and mounts Charlton and Unwin.

4. Back on the main trail, another unsigned junction reached in 200 m leads up to the Opal Peak scrambling route (not described here; see Alan Kane's *Scrambles in the Canadian Rockies* for details). Follow the main trail left and cross a small stream before traversing a stretch of willow flats.

5. Over the next 1.5 km many flowers dot the landscape and views are excellent. Be sure to make plenty of noise coming through this section, as it is a frequent hangout for grizzly bears that can hide quite easily amongst small bumps and troughs.

6. Back in the forest, the trail descends steadily while traversing back towards the junction. There are a few steeper sections and several small rises, but overall expect nice forest with occasional glimpses of mountains to the west. Once back at the junction, turn right and follow the trail back down towards the parking area.

There are great opportunities for wildflower photography while wandering along this trail.

▲ *Distant views across the valley to mountains of the Maligne Range motivate a future journey along the popular Skyline Trail.*

▼ *The return leg of Opal Hills Loop is thankfully much mellower than the ascent.*

14 Bald Hills

One of the best viewpoints overlooking scenic Maligne Lake, Bald Hills is a technically straightforward way to get up into the alpine along an old fire road. Dirt and gravelly trails lead higher up towards a summit and a scenic ridgecrest traverse. This route is a perennial favourite of locals and visitors alike. Neither dogs nor bikes are allowed on this trail.

DISTANCE: 13.5 KM

HEIGHT GAIN: 700 METRES

HIGH POINT: 2380 METRES

MODERATE

MID-JULY TO THE END OF SEPTEMBER. This area is often subject to closures or restrictions in July and August due to grizzly bear activity.

Start: From the junction of Hwys 93 and 16 near Jasper, travel east on Hwy 16 for 6 km before turning right onto Maligne Road and crossing the Athabasca River. Stay on Maligne Road for 44 km, following signage for Maligne Lake, passing the day lodge and crossing over the outflow of Maligne Lake. The parking area is on the left at the end of the road.

Difficulty: Good travel on well-maintained trail. The first leg of the route ascends as old gravel road before veering onto steep terrain (which can also be quite rooted). Once in the alpine, travel is mellow and pleasant. Plan on taking more time than the distance and height gain values suggest, to soak up the sublime sights.

1. Leave the parking area from its southwest side, where a trailhead kiosk marks the start of a wide, gated road with signage for trail 23. This former fire road starts gently gaining elevation, passing horse hitching rails and a signed junction with the Moose Lake loop (stay straight on the main road). Just past the junction, a broad clearing on the right is home to the Maligne Lake weather station and an old Lovat Scouts camp.

The trails starts as an old gravel fire road and steadily winds its way upwards to the alpine.

Keep an eye open for the hiker trail (left), which is the recommended route for the ascent.

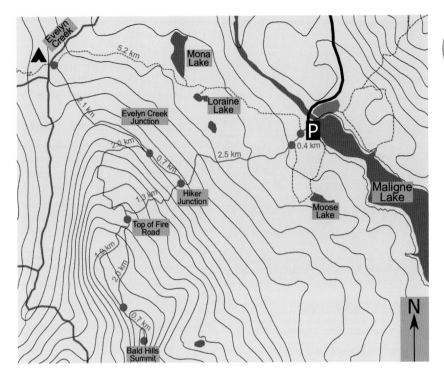

2. The road ascends and in 2.5 km reaches a signed hiker junction. The narrow hiker trail climbs quite steeply up into the alpine, while the more mellow road reaches the same point in double the distance. It is recommended to take the hiker trail on ascent and return via the road.

3. As the trail gains elevation, on a somewhat rocky and rooty footing, views towards Maligne Lake steadily improve. There are many gaps in the forest that make for great photos as well as being opportunities to catch your breath. After 1.25 km the trail reaches a junction on the edge of treeline.

Near the top of the hiker trail there are numerous excellent viewpoints towards Maligne Lake and the rest of the Maligne Valley.

▲ *Snow patches can linger on the Bald Hills trail until July some years. The trail works towards the south summit, visible in the distance left of centre.*

▼ *Outstanding views looking north from the summit of Bald Hills. The rest of the loop follows the ridgecrest at left in the photo before descending back to the fire road.*

If looking for a shorter day, turn right, which will link up with the old road and make a loop. Otherwise, turn left and follow the trail for 400 m to another junction. Turn left again, now heading south along a gently rising trail that leads to the true summit of Bald Hills.

4.   Keep following the established trail for 1.5 km as it moves into the alpine with wide-reaching views and often a refreshing breeze. Turn left at a final junction to head towards the summit. When two small rocky bumps are encountered just below the summit, follow a faint path on the right.

5. When you have finished snapping pictures, return to the previous junction and continue along the ridgecrest towards the more northerly summit of Bald Hills. It is 1.5 km of fabulous ridgetop hiking to reach the northern summit, after which the trail descends steeply back to the treeline junction.

6.   To save your knees some strain, it is recommended to take the old road back

down rather than descending the hiker's trail. About 2 km down the road there is a signed junction towards the Skyline Trail and Evelyn Creek. This extension is described below but will add considerable time and distance to your day if chosen.

FROM TOP *Looking south from the true summit of Bald Hills towards a sea of peaks; Atop the ridge can be an austere environment, with only a few hardy plants clinging to the rocks. Look for yellow markers to point the way down.*

◄ *There are more good views to be had along the fire road during descent, here looking north towards the Skyline Trail and Little Shovel Pass.*

Going farther: Evelyn Connector to Mona and Lorraine lakes

If you're looking for a longer day than the normal Bald Hills loop, there is a handy connector that links up to the Skyline trail near Evelyn Creek to expand the Bald Hills loop to include Mona and Lorraine lakes. For more information, see the trail description for Little Shovel Pass on page 73.

DISTANCE: ADD 8.1 KM (CONNECTOR TRAIL, MONA AND LORRAINE LAKES TO THE TRAILHEAD)

HEIGHT GAIN: ADD 80 METRES (CONNECTOR TRAIL, MONA AND LORRAINE LAKES TO THE TRAILHEAD)

HIGH POINT: 1990 METRES

1. The connector trail, itself an old road, has not been maintained as earnestly as the main Bald Hills fire road and can be quite bushy in places. The first 1 km is mostly flat with small undulations. The latter 1.1 km descends 80 vertical metres, with several short steep sections, until it reaches the Skyline Trail just before crossing Evelyn Creek. The Evelyn Creek campground, immediately on the other side of the creek, makes for a good break spot. Otherwise, turn right to head towards Mona Lake. The wide, well-maintained trail leads back to the parking area.

▼ *Carry on down the Bald Hills road until you reach the signed junction shown here.*

▼▼ *The Evelyn connector can be a bit overgrown in places but allows for a nice full-day loop.*

15 Little Shovel Pass

The first pass encountered on Jasper's popular Skyline Trail. Hikers can take advantage of light backpacks to reach the pass and take in the views as a day trip with worthwhile detours to Mona and Lorraine lakes along the way.

DISTANCE: 24.5 KM

HEIGHT GAIN: 750 METRES

HIGH POINT: 2240 METRES

MODERATE

MID-JULY TO THE END OF SEPTEMBER.

▲ *The start of the Skyline Trail is easy to follow as it weaves through pleasant forest.*

Start: From the junction of Hwys 93 and 16 near Jasper, travel east on Hwy 16 for 6 km before turning right onto Maligne Road and crossing the Athabasca River. Stay on Maligne Road for 44 km, following signage for Maligne Lake, passing the day lodge and crossing over the outflow of Maligne Lake. Parking is on the left, at the end of the road.

Difficulty: Straightforward travel on a well-maintained and well-graded trail. Expect a few isolated muddy patches, especially near the pass in the early summer.

1. Exit the parking area from its west side, following a well-worn trail that crosses Maligne Lake Road. There are two trailhead kiosks visible. Take the one on the

right to follow signage for the Skyline Trail (also known as trail 100). One of the most notable features along the first stretch are kettles (holes left behind by chunks of glacial ice deposited by passing glaciers). Some kettles are dry, while others are tiny lakes.

2. At 2.1 km from the trailhead there is a junction for Lorraine Lake. It is worthwhile taking a detour here (400 m return, descending to a smaller shallow lake and

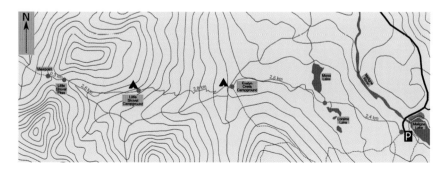

▲ Looking across Lorraine Lake, Mount Charlton (left) and Mount Unwin (centre) are visible in the distance.

▼ Picturesque Mona Lake is a worthwhile detour. The Opal Hills can be seen in the background.

After crossing Evelyn Creek the trail continues and mountain views abound.

crossing over a short bridge), before continuing on to Lorraine Lake.

3. Some 300 m past the Lorraine Lake junction, you'll come to the Mona Lake junction. This is another fine viewpoint (also 400 m return), though the path to the lakeshore can often be quite muddy.

4. The trail continues for 2.6 km before crossing over Evelyn Creek, with the Evelyn Creek campground on the far side of the bridge. A series of switchbacks gains elevation with intermittent views across the valley before reaching the Little Shovel campground (a great place for a break).

FROM TOP Looking across the valley to unnamed peaks rising above Evelyn Pass as the trail nears Little Shovel Pass; Near Little Shovel Pass looking south, back towards Maligne Lake.

5. From the Little Shovel campground it is a further 2.6 km and 200 vertical metres to reach Little Shovel Pass. The trail continues gently climbing over the next 1 km before emerging into the alpine.

6. The trail meanders through the lowest part of the pass and can be quite soggy after heavy rainfall. A Parks Canada sign proclaims the pass to be at 2240 metres elevation. It is worthwhile to continue another 250 m along the Skyline Trail to get better views towards the scenic Snowbowl Valley to the north.

7. Retrace your steps back to the parking area.

▼ *Take care to stay on the trail in this fragile alpine environment. Little Shovel Pass is almost visible left of centre, with "Sunset Peak" to the right.*

▼▼ *North of Little Shovel Pass the Skyline Trail continues into the valley known as The Snowbowl.*

16 Jacques Lake and Summit Lakes

Less busy than the routes directly beside Maligne Lake, the Jacques Lake trail offers a variety of terrain, culminating in the pristine and placid Jacques Lake itself. While best enjoyed as an overnight trip at the Jacques Lake campground, a ramble to the lake for lunch can be a nice day out, particularly when bikes are used for the first 5 km of old fire road. Beaver Lake (only 1.5 km down the trail) and First Summit Lake (only 5 km) are also worthwhile wanders if out for a shorter day.

DISTANCE: 24.4 KM

HEIGHT GAIN: 360 METRES

HIGH POINT: 1550 METRES

MODERATE

MID-JUNE TO THE END OF SEPTEMBER

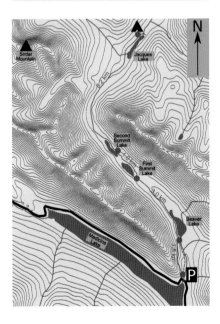

Start: From the junction of Hwys 93 and 16 near Jasper, travel east on Hwy 16 for 6 km before turning right onto Maligne Lake Road and crossing the Athabasca River. Continue on Maligne Lake Road for 27 km, following signage for the lake. The trailhead is on the east side of the road after driving around Medicine Lake.

Difficulty: Expect a mixture of trail conditions. The first leg (following a signed detour) can be muddy and rubbly with one shallow stream crossing. The trail then joins an old gravel road with a few rubbly sections. After First Summit Lake the trail narrows and can be muddy in places, with several shallow stream crossings.

1. The trail starts at the Jacques Lake day use area (complete with washroom and fire pits for a pre- or post-trip BBQ). Extensive trail work in 2022 and 2023 created a new summer trail that leaves the parking area to the north and weaves through the forest. The summer trail crosses at the base of an open avalanche path to avoid crossing side streams of Beaver Creek. If travelling to Jacques Lake during avalanche season (winter and into spring), take the lower trail leaving from the eastern edge of the parking area.

▼ *The recently constructed summer trail avoids crossing Beaver Creek and instead traverses beneath an open rock slope.*

▼▼ *This old fire road wanders through tranquil Rockies forest and makes for easy travel.*

2. Once the trail rejoins the old fire road, travel becomes more consistent. At 1.5 km from the trailhead, you arrive at the south shore of Beaver Lake, with its boat launch and picturesque views northwards across the lake. This is a great rest stop, but you might also find it worthwhile to continue another 150 m north, where there is a small lakeside clearing complete with a picnic table.

3. Some 3 km of easy forest travel leads to a junction on the south side of First Summit Lake. Carry on to the lakeside viewpoint or continue on to Jacques Lake. Travel to Jacques Lake becomes rougher and the trail narrows.

4. After reaching the signed Second Summit Lake viewpoint, the trail becomes more wild with muddy sections and two short, rocky steps making up the final 6.2 km to reach the northeast shore of Jacques Lake.

▼ *The boat launch at the south end of Beaver Lake has impressive views up towards an unnamed ridge that's part of the Queen Elizabeth Range.*

▲ The junction between First Summit Lake viewpoint path (left) and the Jacques Lake trail (right) marks the end of the old fire road.

▼ While much of the Jacques Lake trail travels through forest, there are also lovely viewpoints along the way.

Whilst wandering, keep an eye on the direction of the water flow beside the trail, as the route crosses over a gentle divide into the Rocky River drainage.

5. From the Jacques Lake campground, it is worthwhile to carry on for 300 m, crossing a bridge over the outflow of Jacques Lake to reach the Rocky Forks warden cabin (recently converted into a winter-only hut operated by the Alpine Club of Canada). A short meander from the cabin back towards Jacques Lake gives a great view of the surrounding mountains, the lake and often waterfowl as well.

6. After a good lunch, and perhaps an invigorating swim in the lake, return the way you came.

▲ An old horse gate along the shore of Jacques Lake marks the boundary of the Jacques Lake campground.

▼ The northeast shore of Jacques Lake by the warden cabin boasts an excellent view.

17 Watchtower Basin

Known to most as a side trip along the Skyline Trail, Watchtower Basin is actually a scenic destination and far less busy than other trails in the neighbourhood. A 2015 wildfire that started at nearby Excelsior Creek scorched the first leg of this trail. This route should be avoided during periods of strong winds, as there are still many standing dead trees along the first 2.4 km. Neither dogs nor bikes are allowed on this trail.

DISTANCE: 18.6 KM

HEIGHT GAIN: 700 METRES

HIGH POINT: 2010 METRES

STRENUOUS

LATE JULY TO THE END OF SEPTEMBER.

Start: From the junction of Hwys 93 and 16 near Jasper, travel east on Hwy 16 for 6 km before turning right onto Maligne Lake Road and crossing the Athabasca River. Stay on Maligne Lake Road for 18 km, following signage for the lake, then turn right into a large unsigned parking area beside the Maligne River.

Difficulty: Interesting and varied travel along an adventurously less maintained trail. Expect muddy and overgrown sections, especially once the trail parallels Watchtower Creek. Packing a pair of stream-crossing shoes may be useful for unbridged crossings of both the Maligne River and Watchtower Creek.

1. As you leave the trailhead the first challenge of this route is to cross the Maligne River. Stream-crossing shoes are advantageous, as there is no longer a bridge over the Maligne River. During periods of intense rainfall the river may be outright impassable. Plan your crossing carefully and be wary of slippery, water-worn rock surfaces underfoot. Once on the west side, follow

yellow diamond markers as the trail works its way up through open burned forest.

2. At 1.7 km from the road, the trail crosses an unnamed creek amidst a brief island of intact forest. After the creek, there is another 600 m stretch of burned forest before returning to more conventional, and often moist, travel for the rest of the route. The trail climbs several sustained steep sections before traversing into the Watchtower Creek valley.

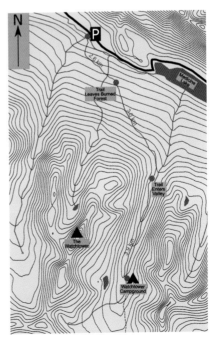

3. At 5.6 km from the road, the trail reaches Watchtower Creek and there are great mountain views to be seen. The ensuing 3.7 km can be muddy and difficult to follow in places, but it is well signed where less distinct. The trail generally stays within 20 m of the creek. Large yellow-diamond markers show the designated crossing point to reach the Watchtower campground (see page 84), which is a great place for a break to enjoy the scenery.

4. If time and energy permit, a better-defined trail continues southwards from the campground for just over 3 km before linking up with the main Skyline Trail near Big Shovel Pass. Retrace your steps back to the parking area.

▼ *The trail starts at the edge of the parking area and heads up towards the burned forest.*

▼▼ *The unbridged crossing of the Maligne River shown here is usually straightforward during the summer, except during sustained periods of heat or heavy rainfall.*

▲ The burned forest glows pink with fireweed during the summer months.

◄ The trail becomes much more defined after leaving the burned forest, and travel is easier.

◄ After entering the Watchtower Valley, the trail can become overgrown but wildflowers abound.

▼ Watchtower Creek bubbles beside the trail, with distant views towards Big Shovel Pass to the right.

▼▼ Excellent views and sublime mountain ambience are abundant in the Watchtower basin. The crossing point to reach the Watchtower campground is visible right of centre, at the red dot.

18 Signal Mountain Lookout

There are few better viewpoints around the Jasper townsite than atop Signal Mountain Lookout. While technically straightforward, this trail is long and sustained in its elevation gain. Save this route for a clear day when views from the top will be magnificent. It is recommended to get an early start to avoid trudging up during the heat of the afternoon sun. In dry years, seasonal creeks described below will likely have disappeared, so bring plenty of water. Dogs are not allowed on this trail, and bikes are permitted only as far as the Skyline Trail junction.

DISTANCE: 18.5 KM

HEIGHT GAIN: 975 METRES

HIGH POINT: 2110 METRES

MODERATE

EARLY JULY TO THE END OF SEPTEMBER

The trail starts out mellow and wide but soon starts to gain elevation.

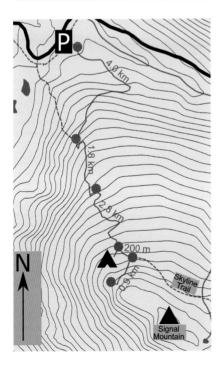

Start: From the junction of Hwys 93 and 16 near Jasper, travel east on Hwy 16 for 6 km before turning right onto Maligne Lake Road and crossing the Athabasca River. Stay on Maligne Lake Road for 5.5 km, following signage for the lake, before turning right into a small parking area indicated by a hiker symbol.

Difficulty: Straightforward travel on an old gravel road. Snow patches can linger along the upper third of the route until mid-July.

▲ *When having a break on the sustained climb, don't forget to look behind you for mountain views.*

► *Nearing the end of the road there are great views north to the Victoria Cross Ranges. The distinctive peak on the left is Mount Bridgland.*

▼ *Bike racks mark the junction with Skyline Trail. The distinctive form of Roche Bonhomme ("Old Man Mountain") can be seen across the valley to the east.*

1. Leaving the parking area the trail is wide and mellow, a great way to warm up your legs for the climb to come. After the first 1 km, the road steepens and steadily winds upwards, eventually reaching a junction with trail 7i (stay straight on the road).

2. At 1.5 km past the junction, there is a nice flat spot for a break near a seasonal creek. After this the grade steepens again, and there is still almost 500 metres of elevation to climb! The trail becomes rockier, with a few perennial muddy patches. When the ridge of Signal Mountain starts to come into view you are only a few minutes away from the junction with the Signal campground and the Skyline Trail junction.

▲▲ *The old road becomes more vegetated as the trail approaches treeline. The Athabasca River can be seen at far left, flowing out of Jasper National Park.*

▲ *From just below the lookout there are wide-reaching views down the Athabasca valley and towards peaks of the Colin Range.*

3. Stay right on the wide old road to carry on towards the lookout. The trail soon emerges from the trees to give wide-reaching views and enters the preferred habitat of many hoary marmots. The road ends at a small plateau that is the site of a former fire lookout with an excellent view of the Athabasca River valley, the entire Jasper townsite and peaks near and far.

4. When you have finished admiring the views, work back down the way you came. A benefit of this route is that, on the descent, many of the steeper sections of road have nice views of Pyramid Mountain as well as eastwards towards peaks of the Colin Range.

▲ Fine views of the Jasper townsite and Pyramid Mountain (right), from the top of the lookout trail.

▼ Southwest from the viewpoint, Mount Edith Cavell is visible left of centre, with numerous peaks in the Tonquin Valley visible at centre and right.

19 Maligne Canyon Loop (Bridges 1–6)

There are many ways to experience Maligne Canyon, one of the signature hikes in Jasper National Park. The loop described here carries on to all six bridges to get a feel for the great variety tucked into a small area. Plan on spending more time on this route than the distance suggests, as there is a lot to see!

DISTANCE: 8.0 KM

HEIGHT GAIN: 150 METRES

HIGH POINT: 1150 METRES

EASY

ALL SUMMER SEASON (consider bringing microspikes when snowy)

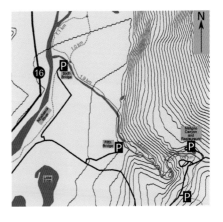

Note: *This map has a contour interval of 20 metres.*

Start: Parking Area 11, Upper Maligne Canyon. From the junction of Hwys 93 and 16 near Jasper, travel east on Hwy 16 for 6 km before turning right onto Maligne Lake Road and crossing the Athabasca River. Stay on this road for just over 6 km, following signage for the lake, before turning left into Parking Area 11, signed for Maligne Canyon.

Difficulty: Straightforward travel on a well-maintained trail. Expect a few steep sections and isolated muddy patches. The trail between Fifth and Sixth bridges is often muddier than the rest of the route.

1. This route starts on the south side of the Maligne Canyon parking area, near the restaurant, and is well-signed with interpretive displays. Along the first 100 m there are fossils embedded in the limestone beneath your feet! A fenced-off viewpoint descends off the main trail and gives a good look down into the narrow and eroded canyon. Once you've regained the main trail, First Bridge is right around the corner.

2. First Bridge is the second-deepest section of Maligne Canyon and sports an amazing waterfall on its east side and an interesting narrow chockstone on its west. About 150 m farther down the trail you come to Second Bridge, over the deepest part of the canyon at 51 metres! Stay on the south side of the river, following signage for trail 7.

3. Leaving Second Bridge, the trail descends on a mix of dirt and some concrete steps. Looking across the canyon the pocketed rock is home to nesting black swifts. A short but steep descent leads to Third Bridge, after which the trail becomes

▲ The upper part of Maligne Canyon has interesting erosion patterns where the Maligne River has wormed its way through the limestone.

◄ Second Bridge over Maligne Canyon spans its deepest section.

FACING PAGE The canyon becomes less deep but more rugged as the trail moves past Third Bridge.

rougher and muddier. When you come to a junction with trail 7f, stay on trail 7.

4. After passing Fourth Bridge there is a dramatic change in water level in the Maligne River. The Maligne valley is home to a geological karst system that acts as a series of supply and drainage pipes, and numerous springs can be seen adding water into the river. As the trail follows the course of the river, numerous rapids can be seen, as well as one particularly notable waterfall known locally as Bridal Veil Falls.

▲ *Throughout the canyon there are numerous underground springs, some quite large as shown here between Fourth and Fifth bridges.*

▼ *This interesting small cascade is known locally as Bridal Veil Falls.*

▲ Approaching Fifth Bridge the canyon has broadened considerably, and underground springs have built the Maligne River into a mighty torrent.

▼ There are several wet sections along the trail between Fifth and Sixth bridges.

5. Between Fourth Bridge and Fifth Bridge the trail rises above the river and grants views of Pyramid Mountain and the Victoria Cross Ranges. The last hill down to Fifth Bridge is steep and can be slippery.

The route to Sixth Bridge turns right at the bottom of this hill (follow signs for trail 7), but it is worthwhile first heading down to Fifth Bridge for some riverside views.

6. Between Fifth and Sixth bridges the trail wanders away from the Maligne River, crossing beneath interesting rock features, spring-fed ponds and a few perennially muddy sections. The trail then returns to the river, with numerous unsigned spur trails granting good views of rapids below and mountains above. After reaching Sixth Bridge, consider the short extension noted below, adding the Flower Loop (trail 10a).

7. To return to the parking area, stay on trail 7f at previously encountered junctions, as it passes higher above the river and grants wider-reaching views. Trail 7f will lead back to the north end of the parking area, completing the loop.

The last section of the trail to reach Sixth Bridge parallels the course of the Maligne River.

Going farther: Flower Loop (trail 10a)

A pleasant ramble along the bank of the Athabasca River, with mountain views and flower finding potential.

DISTANCE: ADD 2.5 KM (SIXTH BRIDGE TO SIXTH BRIDGE)

HEIGHT GAIN: NEGLIGIBLE

HIGH POINT: 1020 METRES

1. From Sixth Bridge stay on the north side of the Maligne River and follow signs for trail 10a. The route soon moves into the forest and in a serpentine fashion approaches the Athabasca River. The track parallels the course of the Athabasca, with unobstructed views and many wildflowers bordering the path. The trail then leaves the main channel of the Athabasca and comes to a junction with Overlander Trail. Turn right to return to Sixth Bridge, passing by a fenced-off Parks Canada compound.

▲ *The Flower Loop travels along the Athabasca River and has fine mountain views.*

Wild chives, shown here, common harebell and wood lilies dot the landscape along the trail.

When working back along the Flower Loop, the trail passes a Parks Canada facility at Sixth Bridge.

EAST OF TOWN

20 Fiddle Pass

Nestled between the foothills and Jasper National Park, Whitehorse Wildland Provincial Park is a beautiful landscape to explore. The hike to Fiddle Pass explores the wide range of terrain in Whitehorn Wildland, including canyons, meadows, forest and, regrettably, some perennially muddy sections. For a shorter day, the route to the Sawmill campground (described below) also makes for a fine trip.

DISTANCE: 26 KM

HEIGHT GAIN: 550 METRES

HIGH POINT: 2120 METRES

STRENUOUS

EARLY JULY TO END OF SEPTEMBER

Start: Whitehorse Creek campground. From the junction of Hwys 93 and 16 near Jasper, travel east on Hwy 16 for 74 km, passing out of Jasper National Park, and turn south on Hwy 40 (signs for Cadomin). Continue south on Hwy 40, some sections of which are gravel, for 48 km (passing through an edge of the decommissioned Luscar coal mine) before turning right, onto Range Road 234A to reach the hamlet of Cadomin. Drive 7.5 km, passing through Cadomin, before turning left at a signed junction for Whitehorse Creek campground. Drive through the campground to reach the trailhead and signed day-use parking area.

Difficulty: This route travels through a wide variety of types of trail. Expect muddy stretches, several unbridged stream crossings, and patches of rubble. Wait until after a long period of dry weather to travel this route.

▼ *Fiddle Pass Trail starts in rolling hills characteristic of the front ranges of the Rocky Mountains.*
▼▼ *The trail follows the course of Whitehorse Creek, with numerous trailside viewpoints.*

1. Leaving the trailhead, the route follows along the north side of Whitehorse Creek, passing by a series of small cascades known as Lower Whitehorse Falls. Stay left, following signage for Lower Whitehorse Trail. Over the next 2 km, the trail winds up and down near Whitehorse Creek, with many great viewpoints. When you reach a junction with Drummond Trail, continue straight on the main trail.

2. The next 2.5 km travels through denser forest and patches of open meadows before passing through Trappers campground and rejoining with the Upper Whitehorse trail. After the campground, the trail emerges into a lovely clearing with distant mountain views. The route then passes the signed Sawmill campground junction, which is a good place for a break. If planning a shorter day, it is worthwhile to turn around here.

▲ Farther up the valley, Whitehorse Creek mellows and striking mountains come into view. Neither of the two peaks visible in the distance, part of the Nikanassin Range, is officially named.

▼ The trail moves into forest as it starts to ascend towards Fiddle Pass.

◄ *Fiddle Pass is a popular destination for horse parties and there are many muddy sections, particularly during periods of heavy rainfall.*

▼ *Once the trail emerges from the trees, Fiddle Pass comes into view. Mount Berry is visible in the distance, to the right of the pass.*

3. Leaving Sawmill campground, the trail crosses over an unnamed creek and passes an unsigned junction with a trail that leads to the Harlequin patrol cabin 300 m off the main trail, in an open clearing with nice views. Follow signage for Fiddle Pass, staying right at several signed junctions. The climb towards Fiddle Pass is steep in places, and after rainfall has many muddy patches of horse-damaged trail. From the Sawmill campground it is just over 5 km and 400 vertical metres to the Fiddle Pass campground, perched at the edge of treeline.

4. From the Fiddle Pass campground the trail passes through a lush alpine bowl with numerous wildflowers and impressive mountain views. A shallow stream crossing and a gentle climb to the pass mark the end of the route. A further 26 km along the trail into Jasper National Park would take you to Miette Hot Springs.

5. Return to the trailhead via the same route.

▲ Looking north from Fiddle Pass into Jasper National Park. Slide Mountain is visible in the distance right of centre.

▼ Fiddle Pass marks the boundary between Whitehorse Wildland Provincial Park and Jasper National Park.

21 Folding Mountain

Straddling the boundary between the foothills and the front ranges, Folding Mountain is a great viewpoint and has a long hiking season. Plan on bringing plenty of water for this route, as there are very few sources along the way.

DISTANCE: 17.4 KM

HEIGHT GAIN: 1050 METRES

HIGH POINT: 2110 METRES

STRENUOUS

LATE JUNE TO EARLY OCTOBER. The last section of the trail to the summit travels through avalanche terrain and should be avoided when it is snowbound.

Start: From the intersection of Hwys 93 and 16 near Jasper, travel 57 km east on Hwy 16 and turn right, onto Folding Mountain Ave., following signs for the Folding Mountain Brewing Company and Jasper Gates Resort. There are several possible parking areas for this route. Recent roadwork has provided for parking along Folding Mountain Ave. If this lot is full, it is also possible to park at the Folding Mountain rest area 1 km west on Hwy 16, though this option requires crossing the highway.

Difficulty: The first section of this route is steep, sustained, and rooted in places. Thankfully, the grade then mellows and follows the ridgecrest through pleasant forest. The last stretch of the trail traverses a rubbly scree slope with one small easy scrambling step.

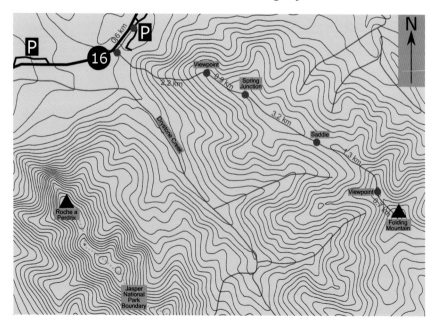

▲▲ The first portion of the trail involves walking along a faint trail beside the highway.

▲ The beginning of the Folding Mountain trail is well-marked, though it can be difficult to spot while driving by on Hwy 16.

◄ To gain the ridgecrest, the trail climbs steadily for 500 vertical metres and has several steep, rooted sections.

There are fine views westward towards Roche à Perdrix as you near the ridgecrest.

1. Starting from the intersection of Folding Mountain Ave. and Hwy 16, travel on ATV tracks paralleling the highway westward for 600 m before reaching a hiker trailhead sign, and well-defined trail.

2. The first 2 km is very steep and sustained, gaining 500 vertical metres. Several sections of exposed roots can be exceptionally slippery when wet. Once near the ridgecrest, the trail passes through open sections with great views west towards Roche à Perdrix and the Athabasca River valley. Stay to the right at a signed junction leading to a seasonal spring.

3. The trail then travels through a mix of dense forest and open clearings before descending to a forested saddle. To reach treeline, the trail climbs a narrow forested rib with fine views east out to the foothills. An open ridgecrest traverse with panoramic views leads towards the summit.

▲ This rocky outcrop is a nice place for a break, looking southwest towards the ridge of Fiddle Peak.

◄ The final segment of the trail travels on steep dirt and scree. In early-season conditions when snowbound, this section can present an avalanche hazard and should be avoided.

4. The summit block is the steepest and most exposed part of the route. A well-worn trail cuts its way up the scree and dirt to gain the final 130 metres of elevation. This part of the route smudges the distinction between a difficult hike and an easy scramble, to cross a short rocky step. Past the step, a good trail leads up to the summit plateau, which can be explored for as long as desired. Take note where the trail reaches the ridgecrest, as you will need to return to this spot on the way back down.

5. Return via the same route. Be careful when descending the steep scree slope of the summit block, especially in wet conditions.

◀ *The technical crux of the route involves passing over the small rocky rib shown here.*

▼ *The summit of Folding Mountain has views of rolling hills to the south and more dramatic mountains to the west.*

22 Sulfur Skyline Trail

Overlooking the eastern edge of Jasper National Park, Sulfur Skyline grants picturesque views of the sea of peaks that are the front ranges. After 750 metres of elevation gain, a soak at Miette Hot Springs makes a great finish for a day in the hills. **Bikes are not allowed on this trail.**

DISTANCE: 8 KM

HEIGHT GAIN: 750 METRES

HIGH POINT: 2050 METRES

MODERATE

MID-JUNE TO THE END OF SEPTEMBER. Miette Road is closed annually from October to May.

Start: Miette Hot Springs parking area. From the intersection of Hwys 93 and 16 near Jasper, travel east on Hwy 16 for 45 km and then turn right, onto Miette Road. Follow Miette Road for 17 km as it works its way up the Sulfur Creek valley and enters the Miette Hot Springs complex. Follow signage for the hikers parking area towards the south side of the facility.

Difficulty: A well-maintained but steep and sustained trail. There are numerous benches along this route that help to break up the climb. Expect a bit of rubbly scree near the summit.

1. From the hikers parking area, head towards the hot springs entrance. The trailhead sign can be seen at the start of a wide paved path leading up into the forest. Pavement continues for the first 400 m, after which you'll have dirt, rocks and roots underfoot.

Older Parks Canada signage near the trailhead refers to Sulfur Skyline as Sulfur Ridge.

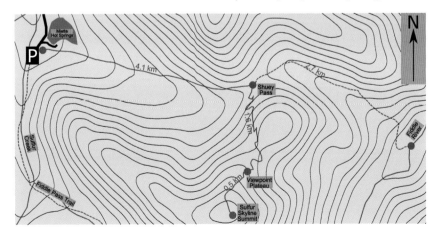

◀ *Shuey Pass is a good place for a break before starting up the steeper next leg of the trail.*

▼ *The sustained switchbacks pay off with fine views north along the Sulfur Creek valley.*

▼▼ *Benches at most of the switchbacks along the climb make this route quite civilized.*

2. The trail gains elevation quickly, with intermittent views through the foliage towards Sulfur Ridge. At 2 km from the trailhead you'll come to a junction, known as Shuey Pass. Turn right and ascend towards Sulfur Skyline.

3. The trail then rises through a sequence of switchbacks. Gaps through the trees start to show excellent views down the Sulfur Creek valley. Benches have been placed at many of the steeper corners along the trail to break up the climb.

4. Some 1.6 km from Shuey Pass the trail rises out of the trees to grant far-reaching views of the surrounding valleys. Stick to the wide, well-established gravel trail as you work your way up the final 140 metres of elevation to the summit.

5. At the summit, there are excellent views all around, and a few established trails allow for short wanders in either direction along the ridge. Be wary of steep drop-offs near the cliff edge, especially towards Mount Utopia! Do not attempt to descend the ridgecrest back to the parking area, as there are many cliffs and other hazards making the route impassable.

6. When you have finished snapping pictures, retrace your steps back to the parking area.

▲▲ *At treeline, wildflowers dot the landscape and the summit is in sight.*

▲ *There are spectacular views in every direction as the trail completes its final switchbacks.*

▲▲ *View from the summit of Sulfur Skyline, looking southwest up the Fiddle River.*

▲ *Moss campion and white mountain avens cling to the alpine terrain at the summit.*

Going farther: Fiddle River via Mystery Lake Trail

For strong hikers with extra energy on the way down from Sulfur Skyline, the first section of the Mystery Lake trail is an interesting trek leading to a nice riverside spot for lunch. Note that from the junction with Sulfur Skyline Trail, this route descends 350 vertical metres, so you will have to regain that amount to get back to your car! Reaching Mystery Lake itself requires fording the Fiddle River and is neither recommended nor described here.

DISTANCE: ADD 5.2 KM (SHUEY PASS TO SHUEY PASS)

HEIGHT GAIN: ADD 350 METRES (SHUEY PASS TO SHUEY PASS)

HIGH POINT: 1670 METRES

1. From the Mystery Lake/Sulfur Skyline junction the trail descends, weaving its way through some encroaching vegetation. Some 300 m from the junction, persevere through a thick patch of willows (take heart: it's only 50 m) until the trail descends more steeply before coming to a small, flat, rocky section (look for orange flagging if the trail is not obvious).

This dense section of willows looks quite fearsome but is thankfully very short-lived.

2. The trail continues to descend as the roar of the Fiddle River can be heard. The last 150 metres of vertical descent consists of steep switchbacks with nice views of the river and surrounding mountains.

3. At the base of the hill, you'll come to a signed junction. Turn left towards Mystery Lake, and within 100 m the trail emerges beside the river at a great place for lunch. Do not continue on towards Mystery Lake, as that requires fording the Fiddle River and

the trail becomes much less civilized. When you have finished your lunch, work your way back up the hill to the Sulfur Skyline junction and back to the hot springs for a well-deserved soak.

▼ *There is quite an interesting array of peaks and canyons down the Fiddle River valley. The outlier of Overturn Mountain is visible in the distance right of centre.*

▼▼ *The Mystery Lake trail continues along the Fiddle River, crossing it twice, and becomes much less travelled after this lovely viewpoint.*

23 Morro Peak

A relatively short but quite steep route to an excellent viewpoint, Morro Peak is popular with hikers and rock climbers alike. The hiker's trail up the peak has improved considerably over the past few years, but keep an eye open for flagging tape and orange-diamond markers at any confusing junctions. Several small rocky steps are encountered along this route that blur the line between difficult hiking and easy scrambling. This trail gets a great deal of afternoon sun, so bring plenty of water, as it can be difficult to find on the route.

DISTANCE: 6.8 KM

HEIGHT GAIN: 700 METRES

HIGH POINT: 1670 METRES

STRENUOUS

EARLY JUNE TO THE START OF OCTOBER

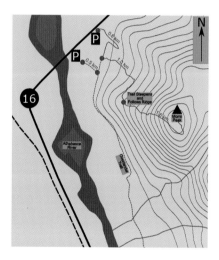

Start: Parking Area 9, the North Overlander Trail trailhead. From the intersection of Hwys 93 and 16 near Jasper, travel east on Hwy 16 for 23 km. The trailhead is in a large parking area 200 m after the bridge over the Athabasca River. It is also possible to start this route from the smaller parking area directly beside the river.

▼ *The trail emerges from the first section of forest to a fine viewpoint.*

The proper trail for Morro Peak is marked with an artfully crafted wooden sign.

Some sections of the trail can be quite steep, especially when descending.

Difficulty: A steep and sustained trail. Expect rubbly sections that can require careful footwork on descent. Near the summit there are several isolated sections of easy scrambling where a fall would have serious consequences.

1. From the parking area, set off on Overlander Trail, following a short, steep step before moving into the forest and climbing to an open viewpoint. After the viewpoint, the trail traverses towards Morro Peak before reaching a crossroads 800 m from the parking area. Look for a quaint wooden sign labelled Morro Peak on your left and follow the trail upwards.

2. The trail trends uphill with a series of steep switchbacks intermixed with stretches of mellower forest. Be sure to stick on the main and most established trail, as there are several spurs heading off into the bush.

▼ *Partway up the trail the inflow of the Snaring River can be seen. Note the different colour of the water compared to the wider Athabasca River, due to having a different amount of glacial sediment suspended in it.*

▲ *Higher up, travel becomes rockier as the trail clings near the edge of Morro Peak.*

▼ *The trail carefully winds to the far side of Morro Peak to avoid the sheer cliff face above. Look for pink flagging tape where the path is fainter.*

Near the summit there are several brief sections of tiptoeing up short, rocky steps.

3. Some 600 m from the Morro Peak sign, the trail traverses southwestwards, wrapping around the peak. At several small descents look for flagging tape marking the correct path.

4. As the trail continues upwards it steepens and several short (1–2 m) rocky steps of easy scrambling are encountered. If you come across any longer or more sustained rock steps, you are likely off route. Turn around and regain the trail, keeping an eye out for markers and flagging tape. The trail progresses through a series of short switchbacks to avoid steep rocky slabs and eventually moves back into a patch of sparse forest.

5. As the trail approaches the summit a large cliff menaces above. Don't worry, the route doesn't ascend this cliff. Instead it wraps around to the southeast side of the summit plateau. For the final 300 m, stick on the easiest terrain, following flagging tape (see photos) before emerging just beneath the summit, where a wide trail leads towards a prominent summit cross and register.

6. On descent, pay close attention to following the same route as on the ascent. Use caution coming down steep, rubbly slopes.

Great views from the summit of Morro Peak across the Athabasca River valley.

FROM TOP *The riverside parking area trail (trail 10b, left) and the main route (trail 10, centre) combine at this scenic junction; There are several short rocky steps along the trail; The northern section of Overlander Trail has many fine viewpoints along the Athabasca valley.*

24 Overlander Trail

One of the most travelled hikes east of the Jasper townsite, this is an excellent way to enjoy the scenery of the Athabasca River valley. The route is described as a traverse from north to south, and staging a car at each end is recommended. This trail has become popular with mountain bikers.

DISTANCE: 15 KM ONE WAY

HEIGHT GAIN: 400 METRES ONE WAY

HIGH POINT: 1260 METRES

MODERATE

MID-MAY TO MID-OCTOBER

Start: Northern trailhead: North Overlander Trail, parking area 9. From the intersection of Hwys 93 and 16 near Jasper, travel east on Hwy 16 for 23 km. The trailhead is in a large parking area 200 m after the bridge over the Athabasca River. It is also possible to start this route from the parking area directly beside the river by following signage for trail 10b.

Southern trailhead: Sixth Bridge parking area 8. From the junction of Hwys 93 and 16 outside the Jasper townsite, travel east on Hwy 16 for 6 km before turning right onto Maligne Road and crossing the Athabasca River. Stay on Maligne Road for 2 km, then turn left to follow signage for Sixth Bridge.

Difficulty: This varied trail travels through mellow sections of forest, across steep rubbly hills, and over a few short, rocky steps. Early in the summer or in other high water periods, the southern end of the trail can be quite muddy.

1. The trail starts on the south side of the parking area with a large trailhead kiosk. Leaving the parking area, the trail quickly gains elevation on a dirt slope before plunging into the forest. Stay straight at two

junctions, the first for the Morro Peak trail, then the second where the Overlander Trail (trail 10) merges with trail 10b. A collection of spur trails dot the left edge of the main route. These lead to rock-climbing areas on Morro Peak and should be avoided.

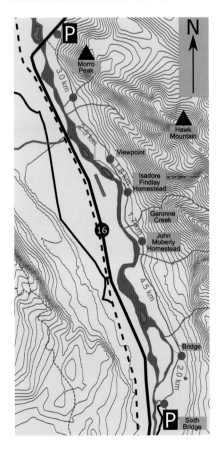

▲ *Looking across the Athabasca River to peaks bordering the Snaring River (at left).*

▼ *The open grassy site of the John Moberly Homestead is a great place for a break.*

2. Keep working your way southwards, admiring the views of the Athabasca River valley. Imagine how wild this area must have felt to the Overlander homesteading families walking this route before there was any highway, railway or other modern amenities. The undulating trail weaves its way through the forest and up a couple of short rocky steps to reach an unbridged crossing of Morro Creek.

3. The trail then traverses a series of flat, forested benches broken up by steep climbs and descents. After climbing a particularly steep hill, the trail punches out of the foliage to an excellent flat viewpoint 5.5 km from the parking area.

▲ The southern part of Overlander Trail travels through many sections of grassy forest and is very pleasant walking.

▼ Near its southern terminus the Overlander passes by a side-channel of the Athabasca River that can often be muddy.

4. From the viewpoint, the trail descends, moving through grassland and willows to reach an interpretive sign at the site of the former Isadore and Philomene Findlay homestead (a family who lived here from 1902 to 1910). Dense forest and several un-bridged creek crossings make up the next leg of the trail before emerging into a wide montane meadow containing the John Moberly Homestead. Please be respectful of the ruins of these old homestead struc-tures. A small spur trail leading down to the river from the interpretive sign is a worth-while wander and a good place for a break.

5. From the homestead, good trail in peaceful forest awaits hikers as the route works its way towards a side-channel of the Athabasca and onwards to the Sixth Bridge parking area.

The Overlander trail ends where it crosses over the Maligne River at Sixth Bridge.

25 Celestine and Princess lakes and the Celestine Lake road

An area rich in history, and gateway to Jasper's longest trail (the North Boundary route), the environs of Celestine Lake are a worthwhile trip and offer a variety of photography opportunities. In fall 2022 the Chetamon wildfire altered much of the landscape in this area, including burning through a large section of Celestine Lake Road. The road is now reopened, and the surrounding terrain offers an interesting glimpse into the process of ecological succession. Thankfully, the trail to Celestine Lake was mostly unaffected by the fire and remains a fine place for a summer stroll. **Note:** *the approach to the lake is via the timed one-way Celestine Lake Road, for which a high-clearance vehicle is recommended. See page 123 for details.*

DISTANCE: 13.5 KM

HEIGHT GAIN: 350 METRES

HIGH POINT: 1250 METRES

EASY

LATE MAY TO EARLY OCTOBER.
THE CELESTINE LAKE ROAD IS CLOSED
TO VEHICLES FROM LATE OCTOBER TO
MID-MAY ANNUALLY.

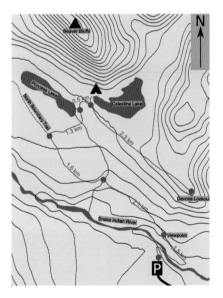

Start: Celestine Lake trailhead, 23 km from the Snaring campsite on Snaring Road. See just next for details.

Difficulty: A wide and mellow trail following an old gravel road. It is quite common to see deadfall lying across the trail if it has not been cleared recently.

The Celestine Lake road is unique in Jasper National Park, as it operates on a time-shared system for one-way traffic. A high-clearance vehicle is recommended. To reach the start of the road from the intersection of Hwys 93 and 16 near Jasper, travel east on Hwy 16 for 14 km and turn

left onto Snaring Road. Follow Snaring Road for 6 km as it crosses over the Snaring River and passes the Snaring overflow campground. From here Snaring Road

FROM TOP *After a short descent, the trail crosses over the Snake Indian River, one of the largest drainages in Jasper National Park; Wide-reaching views to the south along the Rocky River valley. Mount Colin is visible right of centre along with more peaks of the Colin and the Jacques ranges. The eastern extent of 2022's Chetamon wildfire can also be seen; "Cages" like these across the park help ecologists measure the evolving development of the forest.*

changes to a rougher gravel track. Continue on Snaring Road for 8 km until you reach a parking area before an unbridged creek crossing. From this parking area, Snaring Road becomes the timed one-way Celestine Lake road. The schedule is given in the table below. Celestine Lake Road can be quite rough in places, with several exposed corners, and can be an adventure depending on conditions. The Celestine Lake trailhead is reached at the end of the road after 14 km of one-way travel.

1. Congratulations! You have made it to the Celestine Lake trailhead and the eastern terminus of the North Boundary trail. From the trailhead, the path descends to a sturdy bridge over the Snake Indian River. Historically the public was able to drive across this bridge and to within 2 km of Celestine Lake. After the bridge, the trail ascends above the river to a great viewpoint overlooking the Snake Indian River valley.

2. The trail continues deeper into the forest, gradually rising and transitioning into a beautiful stand of trembling aspen. Some 2.5 km from the viewpoint, keep your eyes peeled for an odd-looking "cage" on the right-hand side of the trail. These enclosures are part of a research project across the Jasper National Park region to assess how animal grazing and fire are affecting development of the local flora.

3. The trail continues rambling through peaceful forest before reaching the junction of Celestine Lake Road with North Boundary Trail. Head to the right onto a trail that will rise and fall over several small hills on the way to the Princess Lake viewpoint.

ONE-WAY TRAVEL TO CELESTINE LAKE	ONE-WAY TRAVEL BACK TO HWY 16
0800–0900	0930–1030
1100–1200	1230–1330
1400–1500	1530–1630
1700–1800	1830–1930
2000–2100	2130–2230
2300–2400	0030–0130

The forest around the Celestine Lake road is one of the largest stands of aspen in Jasper National Park.

From the viewpoint, it is only 500 m to the Celestine Lake campground and a nice picnic table for lunch.

4. Retrace your steps back down to the trailhead unless carrying on to the extension up to Devona Lookout (see below). Be sure to time your descent to coincide with one of the scheduled one-way periods for returning to Hwy 16.

▲ *A vintage sign before the junction of the North Boundary trail with the Celestine Lake trail.*

▼ *Princess Lake is just a few steps off the Celestine Lake trail and has impressive views to Roche De Smet (left), Mount Cumnock (centre) and Mount Bistre (right).*

▲ The peaceful waters of Celestine Lake make for a great lunch spot or a good break before climbing to Devona Lookout along the skyline ridge on the right.

▼ After the Celestine Lake junction the trail starts to narrow and the forest becomes dense

Going farther: Devona Lookout

For a little extra effort, the hike up to Devona Lookout rewards visitors with panoramic views and an interesting perspective on the Athabasca River valley.

DISTANCE: ADD 5.6 KM

HEIGHT GAIN: ADD 150 METRES

HIGH POINT: 1390 METRES

1. From the junction before the entrance to the Celestine Lake campground, continue straight, heading upwards. While the trail is wide, travel can be slow due to patches of deadfall. The trail is in dense forest for the first 2 km, after which there are great views of the Athabasca River valley.

2. The high point of the trail is directly beside a weather station, and it's a fine spot for lunch. To get a view eastwards, carry on for 250 m as the route descends, and look for a faint trail in the forest, trending left. Be careful as you work your way down to an unofficial viewpoint, as there is a steep drop just below the viewpoint.

PYRAMID BENCH

26 Pyramid Meadows and Palisade Lookout

Technically straightforward and great exercise, the route up an old fire road to either Palisade Lookout or Pyramid Meadows is a great option for a full-day hike. While either destination makes for a fine trip with excellent views, wildflower enthusiasts should trend towards the open environs of Pyramid Meadows.

DISTANCE: 22.5 KM ROUND TRIP FOR PYRAMID MEADOWS; 22 KM ROUND TRIP FOR PALISADE LOOKOUT

HEIGHT GAIN: 850 METRES FOR PYRAMID MEADOWS; 900 METRES FOR PALISADE LOOKOUT

HIGH POINT: 2000 METRES FOR PYRAMID MEADOWS; 2030 METRES FOR PALISADE LOOKOUT

MODERATE

LATE JUNE TO EARLY OCTOBER

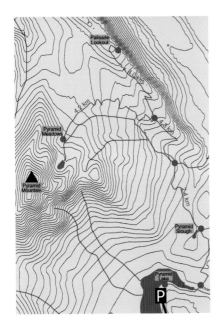

Start: Parking Area 7. From the junction of Pyramid Lake Road and Connaught Drive in Jasper, head up Pyramid Lake Road for 7 km to its gated end on the northern side of Pyramid Lake.

Difficulty: Straightforward wide trail following an old gravel road. Several short, steep hills and brief bushy sections. One unbridged creek crossing near the end of the road before Pyramid Meadows.

1. From the trailhead, step around the gate and skirt the shore of Pyramid Lake along the wide, old road. Enjoy the flat travel in this section, as the sustained climb starts soon! After crossing the bridge over Pyramid Creek, stay straight at the junction with trail 2i, and start climbing. Continue upwards until just past the 3 km trail marker to reach the trailside Pyramid Slough junction.

2. After Pyramid Slough, the trail gently descends to a shallow saddle before numerous switchbacks work ever higher. The grade then mellows and the trail crosses over a wide bridge. An unmarked spur trail just after the bridge (on the right side of the road) grants a great view of Mount Colin. The junction between the Palisades and Pyramid Meadows (known locally as "The Y") is reached 2 km after the bridge.

▲ The trail follows along the shore of Pyramid Lake, with a great viewpoint just after crossing Pyramid Creek.

▼ Pyramid Slough can be a fine place to photograph waterfowl or just take a break while working your way up the trail.

▲ Before reaching the Y junction, there is a great viewpoint looking eastwards to the Colin Range. Mount Colin is the prominent peak on the left.

▼ The last kilometre before the Y junction has excellent views up towards Pyramid Mountain as well as across the valley to the Maligne Range.

◄ The Y junction is aptly named. Pyramid Meadows lies to the left, Palisades Lookout to the right.

The upper portion of the Pyramid fire road winds through many switchbacks but is easy travel.

Going farther: Pyramid Meadows

1. Leaving the Y junction, the trail crosses over a small creek before starting a series of long switchbacks working ever higher. After 2.7 km the switchbacks end and the road straightens towards Pyramid Mountain.

2. Some 200 m before the end of the road, the trail crosses an unbridged creek. It then emerges into Pyramid Meadows, with great mountain views in all directions.

Many opportunities exist to explore the meadows on unofficial spur trails, the best-defined ones heading up towards the right (north) ridge of Pyramid Mountain. Pyramid Mountain itself is often climbed via a scrambling route which is not described here.

3. When you have finished enjoying the picturesque mountain environment, make your way back down the road.

As you near the end of the road, the ridge of Pyramid Mountain comes into view.

⬆ *Pyramid Meadows is a spectacular destination for a day hike. For more far-reaching views, an unofficial trail (part of the Pyramid Mountain scrambling route) winds upwards to the ridge on the right.*

▼ *Looking east from Pyramid Meadows towards peaks of the Colin Range.*

Going still farther:
Palisade Lookout

1. As you leave the Y junction, the trail steadily rises, with long switchbacks making for a comfortable climb. Bands of limestone poke through the old roadbed in many places. Impressive views towards Pyramid Mountain can be seen through gaps in the foliage.

2. At 4 km from the junction, the trail reaches the top of The Palisade. Views improve as you walk southeast along the ridgecrest. Be extremely careful approaching the edge of the ridgecrest, as The Palisade drops off quite precipitously. Be mindful not to damage any of the whitebark pine trees that are scattered about the summit plateau.

3. When finished taking pictures, descend back to the trailhead via the same route.

▲ *Near the top of the lookout trail, there are many places where peaks of the Maligne Range can be seen.*

▲▲ *The Palisade road allows for quick travel but can be a bit overgrown in places.*

◀ At the top of the lookout are numerous whitebark pine trees. These are a protected species and an important part of the ecosystem.

▼ Looking east down the Athabasca River valley from The Palisade lookout.

27 Minnow Lake

A verdant forest hike through the montane environs of Jasper National Park. This trail moves through calm groves of aspen and pine forest while passing four lovely lakes and is a great option for those looking to see flowers and waterfowl. The area around Minnow Lake is home to a population of beavers, and signs of their engineering activities are easy to see. This hike is a good option in the early summer to get your legs back in shape.

DISTANCE: 19.6 KM

HEIGHT GAIN: 550 METRES

HIGH POINT: 1410 METRES

EASY

MID-MAY TO EARLY OCTOBER

Start: Parking area 2, NW corner of the Jasper townsite. Entering the townsite from the east, carry on along Connaught Drive until you reach Pyramid Lake Road. Turn right onto Pyramid Lake Road and follow it until you can turn left onto Bonhomme Street. Drive west on Bonhomme for 1.5 km, following signage for Parking

Area P2, until you come to a small gravel road heading upwards to the right.

Difficulty: Mellow forested trail with a few short hills. West of Caledonia Lake the trail can be quite bushy in places and rain gear is strongly recommended if it has rained recently.

1. From the trailhead, descend following signage for trail 3 to a wide bridge over Cabin Creek. In 150 m turn left at the junction between trail 3 and trail 3e. The route then moves through forest that has been thinned in a forestry practice called Fire-Smarting: removal of highly flammable vegetation to provide an added layer

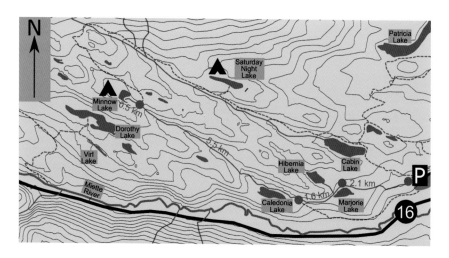

▲ Just after the trailhead, a sturdy bridge crosses over Cabin Creek as the trail weaves its way out of the Jasper townsite.

▼ The forest outside the Jasper townsite has been thinned to reduce fire hazard. A beneficial consequence for hikers is better views of surrounding peaks.

of protection in case of forest fire. When you reach a second junction with trail 3e, continue on trail 3.

2. The trail moves into denser forest over the next 1.5 km to reach a junction with a short spur trail leading to Marjorie Lake. The short 50 m detour down to the shore of Marjorie Lake is very worthwhile, and often during the summer months ducks and loons (along with the occasional other hiker) can be seen enjoying the calm waters. Some 400 m farther along, there is a junction to Hibernia Lake (500 m and a steep climb away). Stay left to stick on trail 3.

3. Undulating aspen forest flows for the next 2 km to reach Caledonia Lake. At a junction with trail 3a, stay right. When Caledonia Lake first comes into view, do not follow spur trails heading to the lakeshore.

The route continues contouring along the north shore of Caledonia Lake, crosses a bubbling brook, and follows some switchbacks to gain a forested rib. This slight change in elevation is enough to alter the character of the forest, and aspen groves fade into lodgepole pine forest.

4. Keep straight ahead at the Minnow Lake junction, where the trail descends to a small campground with picnic tables that makes for a nice snack spot. Keep your eyes open for beaver dams and their builders around Minnow Lake.

5. When you have finished resting your legs, retrace your steps back to the trailhead. It is not recommended to carry on along Saturday Night Lake Loop, as the trail connecting Minnow and Saturday Night lakes is usually muddy and overgrown.

Marjorie Lake is a classic example of a Jasper montane lake. In the distance to the right, rising above the lake, is Muhigan Mountain, while part of Indian Ridge can be seen on the left.

FROM TOP The trail to Minnow Lake has long stretches of denser forest but also a multitude of wildflowers to enjoy; The trail traverses the length of Caledonia Lake before returning to the forest for the final stretch towards Minnow Lake; Much of the trail consists of pleasant walking through lodgepole pine forest; Mountains of the Victoria Cross Ranges soar above Minnow Lake. A large beaver dam can be seen on the far shore, left of centre.

28 Saturday Night Lake

A lovely, forested hike with mountain views, serene lakes and plenty of wildflowers. The trailhead lies within the Jasper townsite, so it's perfect for folks from out of town who want to avoid additional driving.

DISTANCE: 14.5 KM

HEIGHT GAIN: 500 METRES

HIGH POINT: 1420 METRES

MODERATE

MID-MAY TO EARLY OCTOBER

Start: Parking area 2, NW corner of the Jasper townsite. Entering Jasper from the east, carry on along Connaught Drive until you reach Pyramid Lake Road. Turn right onto Pyramid Lake Road and follow it until you can turn left onto Bonhomme Street. Drive west on Bonhomme for 1.5 km until you come to a small gravel road heading upwards to the right, following signage for Parking Area P2.

Difficulty: Well-maintained forested trail with several short steep segments. Early in the year and after rainy periods, expect isolated muddy sections.

1. From the trailhead, hike uphill, following yellow diamond markers for trail 3. Within 20 m the trail turns sharply left and passes an old sign labelled Cabin Lake. The trail climbs steeply with switchbacks to gain the plateau north of Jasper known as the Pyramid Bench. After 500 m, the trail briefly flattens, only to reveal the next hill. No worries, though: this first leg contains most of the elevation gain for the entire route.

2. The trail works its way through open slopes of Pyramid Bench, which are some of the first places near Jasper where paintbrush can be seen in bloom. At a junction with trail 3g, stay on trail 3. After passing a picturesque bench with views south down the Athabasca valley, the trail broadens into an old service road to the Cabin Lake dam. Cabin Lake is the source of drinking water for the community of Jasper. At the

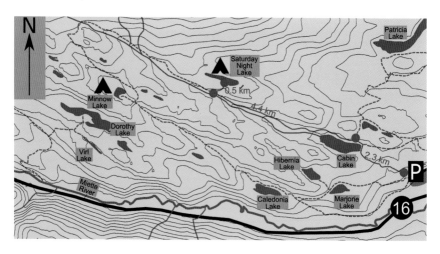

▲ The first stretch of trail is quite steep. Keep your ears and eyes open for mountain bikers, too, who often descend via this route.

▼ Sections of forest on Pyramid Bench have been thinned to reduce fire hazard. Conversely, the reduced density also increases the number and variety of wildflowers.

far end of the dam, turn left, staying on trail 3, which parallels the northern shore of Cabin Lake. As you hike along the lakeshore, many beautiful Douglas firs line the landscape. These aged trees can be great shelter on a rainy day.

3. Leaving Cabin Lake, the trail narrows and descends through stands of lodgepole pine before passing above a wetland bounded by a few steep rocky steps. Large cliffs later appear to the right of the trail, and soon after you'll come to the Saturday Night Lake junction. The last stretch of trail to reach Saturday Night Lakes rises steeply, gaining 40 vertical metres in just 500 m of distance.

4. After enjoying the serenity of Saturday Night Lake, retrace your steps back to the parking area. It is not recommended to continue the Saturday Night Lake loop trail to reach Minnow Lake, as the trail is usually muddy and overgrown.

FROM TOP The trail crosses the dam on the east side of Cabin Lake, with great views towards Pyramid Mountain (right) and other peaks of the Victoria Cross Ranges; The trail works its way above Cabin Lake with fine views across the valley towards The Whistlers.

Wildflowers abound in the forest here, including fields of paintbrush.

Tables nestled beside Saturday Night Lake are a great place for a picnic lunch.

FROM MIDDLE Saturday Night Lake can be a lovely place for waterfowl viewing or a quiet place to read before campers arrive for the evening; Though this is neither the largest nor the highest-elevation lake in the park, there is a calming natural beauty to Saturday Night Lake. Peaks of the Victoria Cross Ranges can be seen rising above.

141

MOUNT ROBSON PROVINCIAL PARK

29 Yellowhead Mountain Trail

A largely forested trail leading up to a great viewpoint perched below Yellowhead Mountain. The lower portions of this route are full of wildflowers. Those who carry on to the trail's end will be rewarded with impressive mountain views. This track can be quite moist in the early summer or after periods of sustained rainfall.

DISTANCE: 13 KM

HEIGHT GAIN: 750 METRES

HIGH POINT: 1810 METRES

STRENUOUS

LATE JUNE TO THE END OF SEPTEMBER

Start: From the intersection of Hwys 93 and 16 near Jasper, travel west on Hwy 16 for 33 km. Just west of the signed turnoff for the Mount Fitzwilliam trail, turn right, onto Lucerne Station Road. A small sign for Yellowhead Mountain Trail can be seen at the start of the road. Continue on Lucerne Station Road for 1.2 km, crossing a bridge over Yellowhead Lake, and park beside the BC Parks kiosk on the east side of the road.

Difficulty: A steep and sustained forested trail. The lower section can be quite bushy, while the upper part passes through wetlands which can be very moist during the early summer.

1. From the kiosk the trailhead can be seen across the railway tracks and is marked with a wooden sign. The first leg of the Yellowhead Mountain trail is quite verdant and can be overgrown if it has not been recently brushed. This section is also a great place to see flowers such as paintbrush, wild rose and columbine. Orange diamond markers point the way ahead. The trail weaves upwards through the forest and crosses over two streams before reaching a bench with excellent views.

From the trailhead kiosk, the start of the trail is marked with a wooden sign which can be seen from across the train tracks.

The viewpoint bench has a fantastic view of Mount Fitzwilliam (left) and Yellowhead Lake.

Much of the trail travels through pleasant lodgepole pine forest and is well marked with orange flagging tape.

2. After the viewpoint, the route moves into denser forest and ascends gradually before emerging into a small wetland with open views of Yellowhead Mountain to the northwest. Orange diamond markers and flagging tape are ubiquitous, and can be helpful where the trail is less distinct. After a short climb the trail crosses another marsh before traversing northeastwards over two seasonal creeks.

3. The upper leg of the route passes above a seasonal creek and through a series of small clearings punctuating pleasant open forest. At the last (and largest) clearing, the trail trends down to a viewpoint of Tête Roche (the name for the northeast peak of Yellowhead Mountain). BC Parks has placed an End of Maintained Trail sign at the edge of the clearing. This area is a prominent

Two wetlands along the trail can make for soggy travel but offer nice views up to Yellowhead Mountain. There are four named peaks on Yellowhead Mountain: from left to right, Bingley, Leather and Lucerne peaks and Tête Roche).

avalanche path, and can be a great place to see glacier lilies in the early summer.

Although the trail ends at this viewpoint, it is possible, and quite enjoyable, to ramble around the open slope towards Tête Roche for better views. Retrace your steps back down to the parking area, taking care when crossing the railway tracks.

▲ There are several unbridged shallow creek crossings along this trail.

▼ Higher up, the trail can become less distinct in sections but it is consistently well marked.

▲ *Vast fields of glacier lilies can be found at the end of the trail in the early summer.*

▼ *The area above the end of the maintained trail offers off-trail exploration opportunities. The rocky summit of Tête Roche rises above.*

30 Fitzwilliam Basin and Rockingham Creek

While more commonly the domain of backpackers, the Mount Fitzwilliam trail offers great day hiking. For a short day, the stroll to the Rockingham Creek campground is worthwhile and grants a fine view of Mount Fitzwilliam. A full and fruitful day can be enjoyed reaching the base of the Fitzwilliam Basin headwall (described below). If aiming to reach the end of the trail at the Fitzwilliam Basin campground, plan for a very early start. It may be worthwhile to pack a pair of trail runners for a perennially soggy wetland you'll encounter halfway along.

DISTANCE: 25 KM

HEIGHT GAIN: 800 METRES

HIGH POINT: 2040 METRES

STRENUOUS

LATE JUNE TO THE END OF SEPTEMBER

Start: From the intersection of Hwys 93 and 16 near Jasper, travel west on Hwy 16 for 32 km, and turn right into the signed Mount Fitzwilliam Trail/Yellowhead Lake parking area.

Difficulty: This route travels through two very different stages. The first, from the

▲ *The first leg of the trail has great views looking north to Yellowhead Mountain.*

▼ *The trail leaves the right-of-way, cutting up into the forest and passing a sign-in kiosk.*

▼▼ *The well-graded trail winds through pleasant forest via a series of switchbacks.*

highway to the Rockingham Creek campground, is a wide, well-maintained trail with several short steep hills. After Rockingham Creek the going becomes rougher, with many unbridged stream crossings and sections of soggy wetland.

1. Leaving the parking area, cross the Yellowhead Highway to find the wooden Mount Fitzwilliam Trail sign where the trail begins. The first leg of the route parallels a pipeline right-of-way for 800 m before reaching a trailhead kiosk that has a BC Parks trail registry booklet. Please take the time to fill out the booklet, as it helps BC Parks gauge usage of the trail and note any required maintenance.

2. From the kiosk the trail weaves upwards along switchbacks with intermittent views westwards prominently featuring Ghita Mountain. The trail then plunges deeper into the forest, gradually gaining elevation but with one notable descent (which serves

Fitzwilliam Creek can be quite deep and swift, especially in the spring.

as a nice break spot) as you work your way towards the Rockingham Creek campground. Rockingham Creek ranges from a raging torrent in the spring to a pleasant bubbling brook later in the fall.

3. After crossing the bridge over Rockingham Creek, the trail becomes rough and travel is considerably slower. The route crests a small hill with many roots and streams while traversing east beneath the gaze of Mount Fitzwilliam. The trail then descends slightly to reach a 2 km stretch of wetland which can be quite soggy, with short sections of indistinct trail (look for orange diamond markers to point the way). The wetland ends with a small rise and the trail weaves on firm ground along the edge of a rockslide.

While the wetland sections can make for soggy boots, there are great views looking up towards Mount Fitzwilliam.

The trail skirts the edge of a prominent rockslide and is marked with yellow and orange diamonds. Mount Fitzwilliam shows a very distinctive change in geology in this view. The upper, darker rock is gog quartzite, while the rock lower down is dolostone.

4. Above the rockslide there are numerous great viewpoints looking up towards the Fitzwilliam Basin headwall. The trail gradually descends towards Fitzwilliam Creek, passing a "2 km to campground" sign. While not a long distance, travel to reach the campground in the upper Fitzwilliam Basin is slow, involving much boulder hopping. The open terrain beside Fitzwilliam Creek makes for a great destination by itself. For a shorter day, turning around here is a good plan.

5. Those who are fleet of foot can hop along boulders, contouring around Fitzwilliam Creek to reach a large yellow trail marker on the edge of the dense forest. The trail climbs upwards, with several unbridged crossings of Fitzwilliam Creek which can be hazardous in high water. The final section of the trail follows alongside the creek before ascending scree and talus in the large gully below Kataka Mountain (look for rock cairns marking the route). Finally, the trail crests over a small ridge to reveal the wonderful alpine environment surrounding the Fitzwilliam Basin campground.

6. When you have finished snapping pictures and gobbling lunch, retrace your steps back to the trailhead.

FROM TOP *Approaching Fitzwilliam Creek, travel becomes quite pleasant, with peaks of the Fitzwilliam Basin towering above; Grassy flats nestled beside the gently flowing Fitzwilliam Creek are a fine destination and a scenic stop for lunch. Aim for the vicinity of the red dot to stay on the trail as it returns into the forest; Fantastic views of the Fitzwilliam Basin from the end of the trail, shown here in mid-June when shady slopes can still be very snowy.*

31 Berg Lake Trail to Whitehorn Shelter

No trail guide to Mount Robson Provincial Park would be complete without a discussion of the Berg Lake trail. One of the most popular routes in the entire Canadian Rockies, the Berg Lake trail is lauded for good reason: it has some of the most spectacular views in the range, pristine lakes, countless waterfalls and of course the towering bulk of Mount Robson itself. From the visitor centre off the Yellowhead Highway, it is over 3000 vertical metres to the summit. **Bikes are allowed until just past the Kinney Lake campground, and horses can occasionally be encountered.**

Note: *A significant rain event in the summer of 2021 led to numerous bridge washouts and trail changes. As of 2022 BC Parks was in the process of permanently rerouting several sections of the trail. Check with the visitor centre to confirm current conditions.*

DISTANCE: 22 KM

HEIGHT GAIN: 300 METRES

HIGH POINT: 1150 METRES

MODERATE

EARLY JUNE TO EARLY OCTOBER

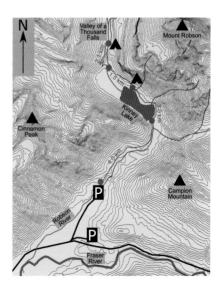

Start: From the intersection of Hwys 93 and 16 near Jasper, travel west on Hwy 16 for 85 km and turn right onto Kinney Lake Road, following signage for the Mount Robson visitor centre. Continue along Kinney Lake Road for 2 km to reach the parking area (a loop at the end of the road, with washrooms and a large picnic shelter). On busy days in the summer, traffic can overflow the parking lot and extend farther down Kinney Lake Road.

Difficulty: Straightforward travel on a very well-maintained trail. Some small rubbly sections and short steep hills.

1. From the parking area, the trail crosses a wide bridge over the Robson River and then passes a double-sided trailhead kiosk. The kiosk's BC side describes Berg Lake Trail, while its Alberta side details Jasper's North Boundary Trail, accessed via Robson Pass north of Berg Lake. The wide dirt trail gently gains elevation as it follows the course of the Robson River. About 1 km along, a short, steep hill marks a large avalanche path descending from Cinnamon Peak.

As you leave the parking area, the trail crosses over the mighty Robson River, with glimpses of Mount Robson towering above.

2. The route winds through a beautiful pocket of rainforest with massive cedar trees towering above, and then returns to the river, with great views of roaring rapids. The shaded forest continues gradually climbing, cresting two small hills before descending the Robson River near the outflow of Kinney Lake. A substantial rain event in 2021 damaged this section of the trail and a short reroute was put in place. Follow orange flagging tape in the rocks on the left side of the trail.

Mountains as large as Robson deviate enormous airflows upward, resulting in cloud formation (a phenomenon called "orographic lift"). This produces intense precipitation along the Berg Lake trail, enabling towering cedar trees to thrive.

3. At the far end of the Kinney Lake outflow bridge there are picnic tables and an outhouse along with a junction between a scenic lakeside loop and the main trail. In periods of high melt or rainfall the lakeside loop can be flooded and should be avoided. Both trails merge after 350 m and then climb three sets of steep switchbacks. Atop the switchbacks, a well-trodden spur trail leads to a fine viewpoint overlooking Kinney Lake.

4. The trail then gradually descends, crossing a short bridge. When you come to a junction with a horse trail, stay left. The hiker trail continues along the lakeshore, reaching the Kinney Lake shelter and campground just less than 7 km from the trailhead.

5. After passing the shelter, the trail crosses a sturdy bridge before coming to Kinney Flats and a junction with the main trail. Bikes are not allowed on Berg Lake Trail after this point (bike racks are

The outflow of Kinney Lake sits at 984 metres elevation, while the summit of Mount Robson towers a further 2970 metres above that.

▲ *Whitehorn Mountain (right of centre) as seen from the lookout above Kinney Lake.*

▼ *The trail crosses the Whitehorn hill through a well-defined avalanche path and can be dangerous during the winter and spring.*

FROM TOP *Looking back towards Kinney Lake from the Whitehorn hill, showing the main Berg Lake trail (centre) and the Kinney Flats optional trail (right); Looking up towards Whitehorn Mountain and Phillips Creek (right of centre) from the Whitehorn shelter.*

Innumerable small waterfalls drip off the slopes of Mount Robson (centre). The two buildings are the Whitehorn ranger cabin (left), and the Whitehorn shelter (right).

provided). While the Kinney Flats route is more direct and has less elevation gain, the flats can become flooded during periods of high melt or rainfall. Look for a sign indicating whether the flats trail is open or closed. If travelling via the flats, follow a wide trail to a series of bridges and look for red-painted sticks. The bridges are sometimes relocated depending on the course of the Robson River, which varies from year to year.

6. From the junction, the main trail climbs 20 vertical metres with small undulations snaking around large boulders before descending steeply to reach the main stem of the Robson River. Two bridges allow passage over the river and onto open gravel flats that grant great views up towards Mount Robson, back towards Kinney Lake and ahead towards Whitehorn Mountain.

7. The main trail travels across gravel flats and merges with the Kinney Flats route just before entering the forest and starting a sustained climb up the Whitehorn hill. It is just under 2 km and 200 metres of elevation gain from the start of the Whitehorn hill to the iconic Whitehorn suspension bridge. At the far end of the bridge, Whitehorn shelter is in sight and there are wonderful views of the picturesque Valley of a Thousand Falls.

8. While the Berg Lake trail continues, its upper reaches are better explored as part of a multi-day trip. Day hiking to the Berg Lake shelter would be a literal marathon, at 42 km round trip. On the way back, it is worthwhile wandering to the Whitehorn ranger cabin on the west side of the Robson River for a better view up towards the summit of Mount Robson.

32 Robson Lookout and Overlander Loop

A nice loop for a short day, particularly if you are staying at one of the nearby campgrounds. This loop sees roaring waterfalls, verdant forest and a scenic lookout with views of both Mount Robson and glaciers in the Cariboo Mountains.

DISTANCE: 9.6 KM

HEIGHT GAIN: 400 METRES

HIGH POINT: 890 METRES

EASY

EARLY JUNE TO EARLY OCTOBER

Start: From the intersection of Hwys 93 and 16 near Jasper, travel west on Hwy 16 for 85 km and then turn right onto Kinney Lake Road, following signage for the Mount Robson visitor centre. At the visitor centre, turn right, into the parking area.

Difficulty: Straightforward travel on mellow, mostly forested trail. Lower sections of the Lookout trail can be bushy in places.

1. The loop is described here going counter-clockwise. Leave the parking area from its west side, passing the Mount Robson café and gas station. Use the crosswalk to reach Hargreaves Road on the south side of the Yellowhead Highway. Continue walking along Hargreaves Road for 650 m until you come to the trailhead sign on the left just before a bridge over the Fraser River.

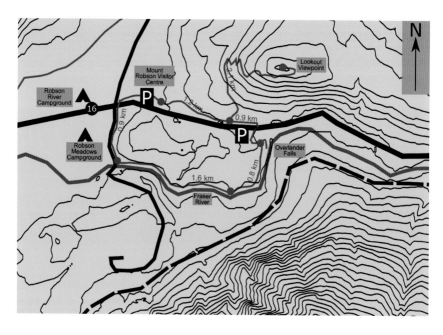

▲ *The Fraser, one of the largest river systems in BC, has its headwaters on the eastern edge of Mount Robson Provincial Park.*

▶ *The trail to Overlander Falls travels through serene sections of forest.*

2. Before setting off on the trail, it is worthwhile to continue 20 m along the old roadbed to a viewpoint on the Fraser River. The trail starts climbing through a tract of private land (which predated the formation of Mount Robson Provincial Park) with several trailside overlooks of Fraser River rapids. A BC Parks interpretive sign shows the location of Hogan's Camp, an outpost during construction of the Grand Trunk Pacific Railway from 1911 to 1914.

3. Carrying on above Hogan's Camp there are more impressive trailside rapids before you reach the signed Overlander Falls junction. Turn right and descend gentle switchbacks to the fenced Overlander Falls viewpoint.

4. Return to the junction, and carry on upwards to the Overlander Falls parking area. Look for a hiker sign across the highway on the northeast side of the parking area. Carefully cross the highway to continue the loop trail as it travels through gentle open forest to reach the lookout junction.

5. Turn right onto the lookout trail, which works its way through several bushy switchbacks before ascending into pleasant open forest. The trail climbs with a steady grade, topping out with a pair of viewpoints, one looking across the valley towards Klapperhorn Mountain and west into the Cariboo Mountains, the other towards Mount Robson and its iconic south glacier.

6. After enjoying the viewpoints, descend back to the lookout junction and continue west along the wide trail. This last section of the loop descends on a narrowing track through denser forest, and passes a water reservoir (servicing the visitor centre) before completing the loop and emerging on the east side of the visitor centre parking area.

FROM TOP Trailside viewpoints give excellent views of rapids along the Fraser River; Overlander Falls is named for a group of settlers, called the Overlanders, who travelled to BC from Ontario in 1862; From the Overlander Falls parking area, the trail crosses the highway and continues to the right of the hill cutaway.

OPPOSITE PAGE FROM TOP Both the lookout trail (right) and main trail (left) are easy to follow; The first lookout viewpoint has fine views of nearby and distant peaks; The second lookout has become more vegetated over the years, but it still grants great views of Mount Robson.

VALEMOUNT

33 Mount Terry Fox via Teepee Creek Trail

In 2020, BC Parks (in collaboration with YORA, the Yellowhead Outdoor Recreation Association) approved a new access to Mount Terry Fox, via Teepee Creek. After several years of work, this trail travels through lush forest and an open alpine paradise to reach the scenic summit. Improvements to the trail are still ongoing, and this is sure to be a favourite destination for locals and visitors alike.

DISTANCE: 16.6 KM

HEIGHT GAIN: 1415 METRES

HIGH POINT: 2630 METRES

STRENUOUS

LATE JULY TO LATE SEPTEMBER

Start: From the intersection of Hwys 93 and 16 near Jasper, travel west on Hwy 16 for 101 km, passing through Mount Robson Provincial Park, then turning south onto Hwy 5 (following signage for Valemount and Kamloops). Drive 13 km south on Hwy 5 and turn left on Tinsley Pit Road (across the highway from the Mount Terry Fox viewpoint). Drive along Tinsley Pit Road for 800 m, crossing a railway track, to reach a signed junction. Turn right at the junction, following hiker signs for Mount Terry Fox Trail, and stay on the main logging road as it climbs 400 vertical metres over the next 4.5 km to reach a large parking area.

▼ *At 1190 metres elevation, the large trailhead parking lot has great views westwards into the Cariboo Mountains.*

▼▼ *The first leg of the trail winds through a bushy, previously forested block with intermittent views up towards Mount Terry Fox.*

Difficulty: A well-laid out trail which can be quite steep in places. Above the Big Rock junction, the route travels on easy scree to reach the ridgecrest. To summit Mount Terry Fox there are short sections of easy scrambling.

1. From the parking area, the route climbs through an old block of logged forest before paralleling the course of Teepee Creek. At 1 km from the trailhead, a bridge crosses Teepee Creek and the trail starts to rise even more steeply. Multiple switchbacks and several short creek crossings work ever

higher through dense forest before reaching a signed junction dividing the Mount Terry Fox Summit and Teepee Lake trails.

2. Turn left onto the Mount Terry Fox Summit trail, which continues climbing through verdant forest as it transitions from montane to subalpine. The trail then travels through a large avalanche path which grants excellent views across the valley. Several small seasonal creeks on the east side of the avalanche path are good places to fill up on water, as the trail above can be quite dry.

Cute bridges such as this one spanning Teepee Creek line the trail.

3. The trail continues climbing towards the alpine, meandering through vast meadows well signed with orange diamond trail markers, before reaching the Big Rock junction. Stay left on the summit trail, which heads upwards following a small band of vegetation towards the scree of the summit ridge.

4. It is 1.4 km and 300 vertical metres from the Big Rock junction to the ridgecrest. Travel can be rough in places and sticking to the marked route will minimize difficulties. Once atop the summit ridge, the route changes character to an off-trail hike with some easy scrambling over scree and talus.

As the trail crosses a wide avalanche path, fireweed dots the landscape and there are excellent views across the valley.

165

▲ The Big Rock shown here marks the junction between the Mount Terry Fox Summit trail and the Teepee Lake connector.

▼ Above treeline the trail can be faint in places, but it is well marked with orange diamonds.

5. There are excellent views in all directions while hiking along ridgecrest to reach the summit. Plan on a lengthy break to soak in the scenery! The final slope before the true summit involves scrambling, so be careful not to dislodge rocks down onto people below.

6. On descent, return the way you came, back to the Big Rock junction. From the junction it is possible to make a loop to also visit Teepee Lake via a steep connector trail (see the route map). This connector trail leaves from the Big Rock junction, but it is quite steep and not described here. Retrace your steps back down the trail to return to the parking area.

▲ Atop the summit ridge, routefinding is straightforward even though there is no defined trail. The true summit is visible in the background.

▼ From the true summit of Mount Terry Fox there are excellent panoramic views, including towards Mount Robson, seen here to the right, piercing the clouds.

34 McKirdy Meadows and viewpoint ridge

Sitting atop the popular Valemount bike park, McKirdy Meadows offers excellent panoramic views of the Cariboo, Monashee and Rockies ranges from a well-maintained trail. There are also opportunities for off-trail rambling on the nearby ridgecrest or a quick lunch stop at the McKirdy cabin.

DISTANCE: 12 KM (VISITING BOTH THE VIEWPOINT RIDGE AND THE CABIN)

HEIGHT GAIN: 675 METRES (VISITING BOTH RIDGE AND CABIN)

HIGH POINT: 2150 METRES

MODERATE

MID-JULY TO LATE SEPTEMBER

Driving up Hillside Road to the trailhead shown here eliminates considerable elevation gain and maximizes time spent in the lovely alpine environment.

Start: A high-clearance vehicle is recommended for reaching this trailhead. From the intersection of Hwys 93 and 16 near Jasper, travel west on Hwy 16 for 101 km, passing through Mount Robson Provincial Park, and turn south onto Hwy 5 (following signage for Valemount and Kamloops). Drive 19 km south on Hwy 5 and turn left into Valemount on Fifth Avenue.

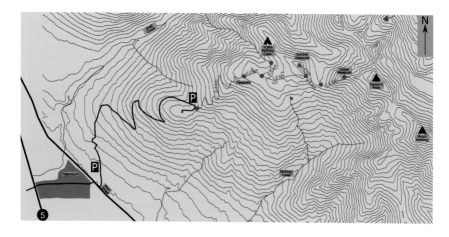

Drive 1.5 km along Fifth Avenue, passing railway tracks, and turn right on Main Street. Within 200 m, turn left onto Hillside Road, following signage for the Valemount bike park. Stay on Hillside Road for 5.7 km as it climbs, quite steeply in places, to gain 700 vertical metres to the signed trailhead.

Difficulty: A well-graded and well-maintained trail. There are several steep hills.

FROM TOP The trail switchbacks, crossing through a gladed trench which gives great views to the west; The higher viewpoint bench gives a bird's-eye perspective of the Kinbasket reservoir. The reservoir was formed from the construction of the Mica dam near Revelstoke, BC, and stretches almost 200 km in length.

1. From the parking area, the trail plunges into dense forest and ascends steep and steady switchbacks. At each of two junctions with an older (and much steeper) trail, stay left. There are several great viewpoints when the trail crosses through a gladed section of open forest. At 2.4 km from the trailhead you come to a viewpoint bench which makes a good place to catch your breath.

2. After a further 1 km of switchbacks, the trail comes to a higher viewpoint bench with an excellent view of the northern end of the Kinbasket reservoir. Higher up, the forest thins and the trail branches, with a signed spur leading to the McKirdy cabin. Visiting the cabin involves a 500 m detour off the main trail, with some elevation loss. The cabin is available for overnight rentals (contact the Cariboo Grill in Valemount for booking), but day use of the covered patio is also permitted. Please be respectful if there are people already in the cabin.

The cozy McKirdy cabin is a welcome sight on a rainy day and a fine destination for an overnight trip.

Working its way across the McKirdy Meadows, the trail ascends to the vegetated ridge above.

3. From back at the cabin junction, the route ascends and crosses through McKirdy Meadows on a well-defined trail. At 1 km from the cabin turnoff, the trail splits to head to either Summit Trail or the viewpoint. Choose left to travel towards the ridgecrest summit.

4. The trail climbs near the ridgecrest for 400 horizontal metres before reaching the summit. It is possible to keep hiking along the ridgecrest to get a variety of views. Return the way you came and consider the extension described below that leads up to a higher viewpoint along the ridge to the south. **Note** that as of 2023 a new trail extension was being built that will carry on northwards along the ridgecrest to allow a loop returning to the cabin. Keep an eye open for orange trail markers pointing the way, but be mindful that this new trail may not be finished yet and may be harder to follow.

The well-planned trail snakes along below the ridgecrest to make for a comfortable grade. The foreground ridge is known as Carson's Ridge, with Mount McKirdy rising in the background.

▲ *This last leg of the trail ascends open slopes with far-reaching views.*

▼ *From the summit of the viewpoint ridge you can see peaks of three ranges: the Rockies to the east, the Cariboos to the west and the Monashees to the south.*

▼ *The view back towards McKirdy Meadows, with the summit of the lookout ridge to the right.*

Going farther: Upper Viewpoint Col

Gaining more elevation, ascending the outlier of Carson's Ridge grants wider views and makes for a full day.

> DISTANCE: ADD 2.8 KM (FROM JUNCTION TO UPPER COL)
>
> HEIGHT GAIN: ADD 375 METRES (FROM JUNCTION TO UPPER COL)
>
> HIGH POINT: 2240 METRES

1. From the branching of the Summit and Viewpoints trails, descend the ridgeline on a well-defined trail for 400 horizontal metres before reaching a flat, forested pass. A new trail allows for straightforward, though steep, travel up to a higher viewpoint. The new trail is still a work in progress and may be indistinct in places, but the route is very well marked with orange flagging tape.

2. Carry on up the ridgecrest as it switchbacks steeply across vegetated and rocky steps to gain 200 vertical metres, reaching a large cairn. If you do not have a head for heights, the cairn is a good place for a break and an excellent viewpoint in its own right. Above the cairn, the flagged trail scampers across rocky benches before traversing on a narrow path across a forested slope to reach a scenic high col. It is possible to continue on towards the summit of Carson's Ridge via a scrambling route that is not described here. When finished enjoying the scenery from the high col, retrace your steps back to the viewpoint junction and head down the main trail.

▲ Partway up the route to the upper viewpoint col, a cairned plateau is an excellent place for a break.

◄ A faint but well-flagged trail traverses the slope to reach the upper viewpoint col.

▼ There are outstanding views from the upper viewpoint col, especially towards Mount Robson, the highest peak in the Canadian Rockies.

Contact Information

Jasper National Park visitor centre

500 Connaught Drive in Jasper
780-852-6176 (visitor centre)
780-852-6177 (backcountry trails office)
780-852-6155 (dispatch)

Mount Robson Provincial Park visitor centre

At the foot of Mount Robson along Hwy 16
250-566-4038 (May 15 to September 30),
250-964-3489 (October 1 to May 14)

Whitehorse Wildland Provincial Park

780-865-8395 (information)

Acknowledgements

The author would like to thank RMB's publisher, Don Gorman; editor Joe Wilderson and designer Gerilee McBride for their help with producing this project. Additional thanks to Katerina Halik for her help and support throughout the writing.

Emergency

DIAL 911

Index

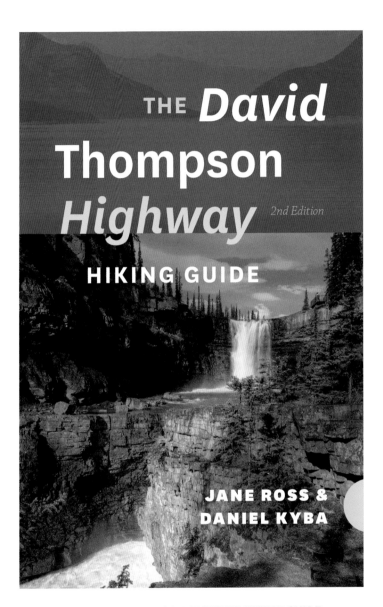

THE *David*
Thompson
Highway 2nd Edition

HIKING GUIDE

JANE ROSS &
DANIEL KYBA

THE DAVID THOMPSON HIGHWAY HIKING GUIDE
2nd Edition

JANE ROSS & DANIEL KYBA
9781771600910

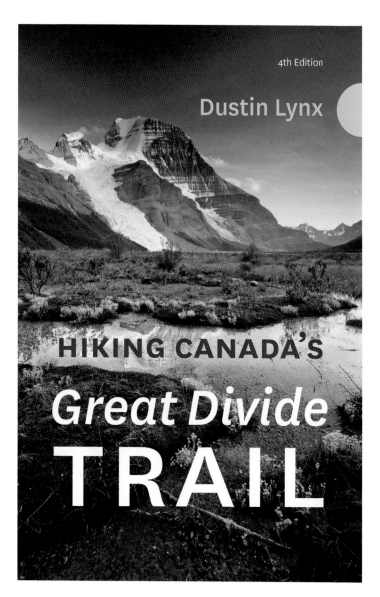

4th Edition

Dustin Lynx

HIKING CANADA'S
Great Divide
TRAIL

HIKING CANADA'S GREAT DIVIDE TRAIL
4th Edition

DUSTIN LYNX
9781771605496